THE QUESTKIDS®

in easy steps
BOOKS FOR KIDS

T0126168

Coding with Scratch

when 🏳 clicked

Create Fantastic Driving Games

when 🏳 go!

move 10 steps   say finished   set speed 50   change

FINIS

Max Wainewright

To create the games in this book you will need:

- a computer or laptop with a proper keyboard — an iPad or any other tablet will not work so well.

- an internet connection to connect to the Scratch website.

It is recommended that children should be supervised when using the internet, especially when using a new website. The publishers and the author cannot be held responsible for the content of the websites referred to in this book.

What is Scratch?

Scratch is a computer programming language that is the easiest language for learning coding, and yet it can be used to create impressive computer games and animations. It is ideal for kids to learn coding and is widely used in schools worldwide.

Scratch is a project of the Scratch Foundation, in collaboration with the Lifelong Kindergarten Group at the MIT Media Lab. It is available to download for free at https://scratch.mit.edu

For further help and resources with this book, visit www.maxw.com or thequestkids.com

The QuestKids® series is an imprint of In Easy Steps Limited
16 Hamilton Terrace, Holly Walk, Leamington Spa,
Warwickshire, United Kingdom CV32 4LY
www.ineasysteps.com
www.thequestkids.com

Copyright © 2022 by In Easy Steps Limited. All rights reserved. No part of this book may be reproduced or transmitted in any form or by any means, electronic or mechanical, including photocopying, recording, or by any information storage or retrieval system, without prior written permission from the publisher.

Trademarks
All trademarks are acknowledged as belonging to their respective companies.

ISBN: 978-1-84078-956-0

MIX
Paper from
responsible sources
FSC® C020837

Printed and bound in the United Kingdom

Notice of Liability
Every effort has been made to ensure that this book contains accurate and current information. However, In Easy Steps Limited and the authors shall not be liable for any loss or damage suffered by readers as a result of any information contained herein.

Contributors:
Author: Max Wainewright
Creative Designer: Jo Cowan
Cover & character illustrations:
Marcelo (The Bright Agency)

Acknowledgements
The publisher would like to thank the following sources for the use of their background illustrations:

Dreamstime, Shutterstock.com

Contents

Coding with Scratch

In this book you will learn how to code your own driving games. If you haven't done much coding before, don't worry – we will cover all the coding concepts you need as we work through the book.

THE SCRATCH SCREEN

Use the **File** menu to save your work.

Switch between editing **Costumes** and adding **Code** or **Sounds** to your sprite.

Click the **green flag** to run your code.

Objects that move around in Scratch are called **Sprites**.

Join Scratch for free or log in to your account.

Your game will run in the area called the **Stage**.

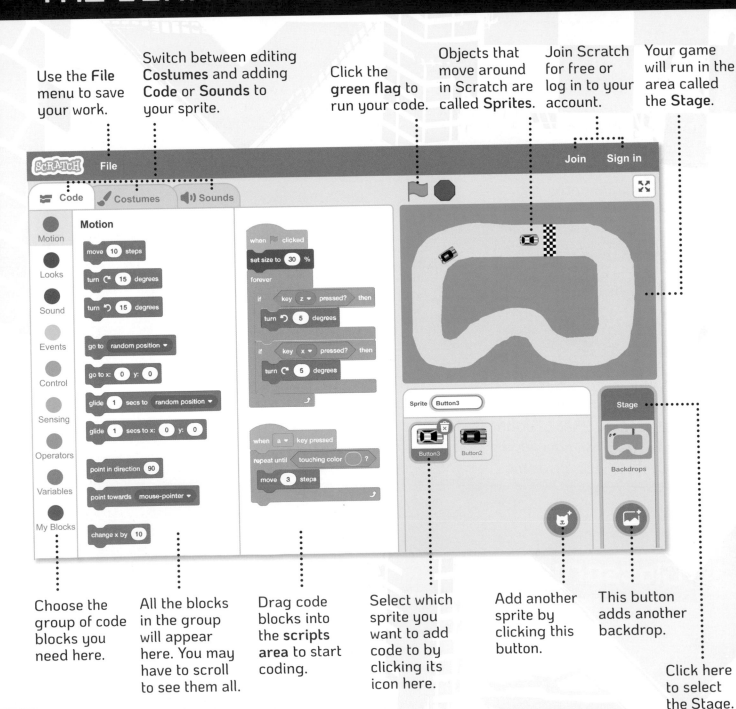

Choose the group of code blocks you need here.

All the blocks in the group will appear here. You may have to scroll to see them all.

Drag code blocks into the **scripts area** to start coding.

Select which sprite you want to add code to by clicking its icon here.

Add another sprite by clicking this button.

This button adds another backdrop.

Click here to select the Stage.

The book will start by teaching you how to code some simple games.

As you progress through the book, the games will get more complex!

You will learn how to create your own car sprites...

...and how to control them with code.

Finding blocks

The colour of the block will tell you which group to look through.

next costume

Motion

Look.

*This block is purple, so you'll find it in the **Looks** group.*

Not all blocks will look exactly the way you need them at first.

touching Sprite1 ▾ ?

*This block isn't in the **Sensing** group...*

touching Mouse-pointer ▾ ?

...so find the block that starts with the same command...

touching Mouse-pointer ▾ ?

mouse-pointer
edge
✓ Sprite1

...and use the drop-down menu.

Joining blocks

Each block in Scratch makes a sprite do something different. To join them together, just drag one block so that it snaps onto another.

next costume

if on edge, bounce

move 10 steps

If you want to break blocks apart, you can't pull the top block up.

You need to drag a block away from the bottom of the stack.

next costume

if on edge, bounce

move 10 steps

Use code to make cars drift around corners!

Learn to make motorbikes do wheelies...

Arranging your code

Most of the games in this block use quite a lot of code. To make the code clearer, it is divided up into different sections or **scripts**.

*Don't try to join the top of curved **event** blocks to other blocks.*

A curved event block is the start of a separate script.

When you have a lot of code, use these controls to zoom in or zoom out of your code.

This button puts your code back to normal size.

Saving your work

You can save your game by downloading a copy of it to your computer.

Click **File > Save to your computer**.

Click **Load from your computer**, then browse to your file to get it back.

Click **File > Load from your computer**.

Saved work is usually found in your Downloads folder.

It's a good idea to save your work after every step.

SAVING ONLINE

It is a little easier to save your work if you have a Scratch account. Your work then gets saved online. This means you can carry on with your work on a different computer. It also allows you to share your completed game. Other people will be allowed to comment on your games too. **Check with an adult before signing up to get a Scratch account.**

Click **Join Scratch** and follow the instructions to create an account.

To log in to your account, click **Sign in**. You'll need your username and password.

Type a name for your game in the box at the top.

Click **File > Save now** to save your work online.

Click the folder icon to see all the files that you have saved (called **My Stuff**).

To load a game to play it or carry on coding, click **See inside**.

Testing your code

After each coding step in this book you will usually see a green flag.

This is reminding you to run your code and check it works. If it doesn't work, check back through the code you have just added. Make sure:

- *You used the correct blocks (some look very similar!).*
- *You have typed in the correct numbers.*
- *You have used minus and plus numbers correctly.*
- ***Loops** and **if then** blocks are in the correct place.*

Sometimes it's a good idea to delete some of your code and start over again.

Later on in this book you'll learn how to add background music to a game.

And how to use variables to keep score and track how fast things move!

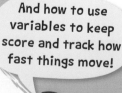

Setting colours

The colour slider lets you pick just over a million different shades.

To help you find the right shade, you will find colour helpers like this one. Set each of the sliders to the numbers shown here.

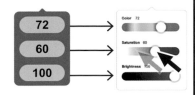

Once you have used a colour, the **Pipette tool** *can be used to "pick up" the exact shade.*

I'll show you how to use the Pipette in your code on page 11.

Drawing backgrounds

Scratch has lots of great, ready-made background pictures called **backdrops**. But for most of the games in this book, you'll be creating your own backdrops. That way, you'll be able to design all sorts of different tracks and levels for your games. Here are some of the tools you will be using:

The **Fill tool** is used to fill in large areas of the screen, such as sky or grass.

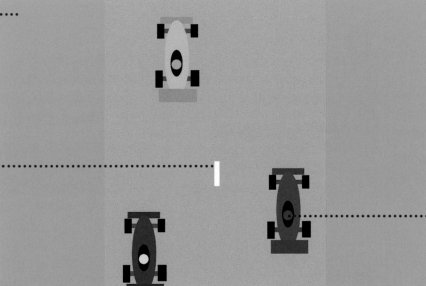

The **Colour tool** is very important. Different colours will tell the sprites whether they are on the track or about to crash!

The **Line tool** can be used to add extra details.

The **Circle tool** can be used to draw ovals or circles.

The **Rectangle tool** is used to draw parts of cars and sections of the ground.

If things go wrong with your backdrop, use the Undo or Redo button.

Undo   Redo

Normal size

Zoom out   Zoom in

Zoom in to add detail to your picture.

BACKDROPS FROM THIS BOOK

If you get really stuck, you can download some backdrops to get you started at www.thequestkids.com or www.maxw.com

Truck Driver

This game will introduce you to the way we will code in this book. We are going to make a simple game where a car drives around a race track. Code will keep the car moving until it crashes into the edge of the track. When the arrow keys are pressed, they will run more code to steer the car. The car will start off as a simple rectangle but you will be able to customise it once the code is running!

1 Start Scratch

Go to the Scratch website.

C **scratch.mit.edu**

2 Start creating

At the top of the page, click **Create**.

Create

3 Make space

There may be a green Help video box. **Close** it to make more space.

4 No cats

We won't need a cat. Click on the bin to delete it.

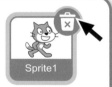
Sprite1

5 New sprite

We need a replacement for the cat, so click **Choose a Sprite**.

> It's in the bottom right of the screen.

6 Find a button!

Scroll through the sprites and click on **Button 3**.

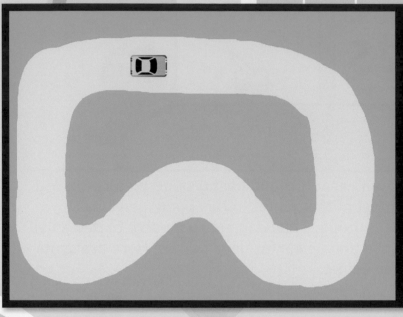
Abby
Ball
Beachball
Button 3

> Once our code is working, we will turn this into an epic car!

7 Start coding!

Drag in these blocks to make the car move when the space key is pressed:

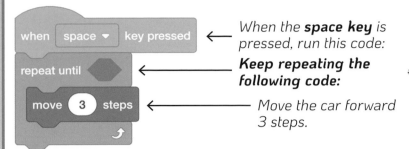

When the **space key** is pressed, run this code:

Keep repeating the following code:

Move the car forward 3 steps.

 Press the big **Space bar** at the bottom of your keyboard to make the car move!

Click the **Stop button** at the top of the screen to stop it.

 Once we have a background, we will tell the code when to stop repeating.

8 Left and right

Add this code to steer the car:

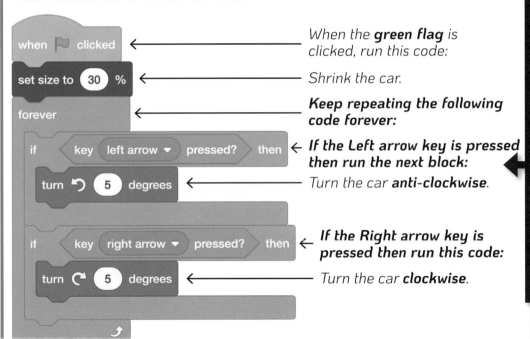

When the **green flag** is clicked, run this code:

Shrink the car.

Keep repeating the following code forever:

If the Left arrow key is pressed then run the next block:

Turn the car **anti-clockwise**.

If the Right arrow key is pressed then run this code:

Turn the car **clockwise**.

COMBINING BLOCKS

Add an **if block** to your code. Drop a **key space pressed block** inside it.

Choose the key you want from the drop-down.

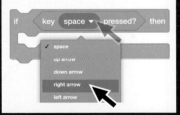

9 Test your code

 Click the **green flag** to test your code. Now, use the arrow keys to make the car turn left or right.

Press the **Space bar** and practice driving around!

 If it doesn't work properly, check your code. Make sure you haven't mixed up the turn blocks.

10 Add a background

Finally, we need to add a background picture for our game.

 Click the **Stage** icon (on the right-hand side of the screen).

 Click the **Backdrops** tab (on the left-hand side of the screen).

 Click on **Convert to Bitmap**. This will give us simpler tools to use.

11 Green grass

Make the whole of the backdrop green.

 Click the **Fill** tool.

Make a green colour.

| 34 |
| 60 |
| 78 |

Fill the Stage in green.

Use these numbers to help mix the colour you need.

12 Ready to draw

Get ready to draw the track.

 Choose the **Brush** tool.

Mix a light grey colour.

| 0 |
| 0 |
| 89 |

 100

Set the brush thickness to 100.

If you make a mistake when drawing, click the Undo button.

13 Draw the track

Carefully draw the track. Choose what shape you want it to be, but keep it fairly simple!

The car should only be able to drive on the road! We need to fix our code to make sure it does.

14 Drive around!

 Click the **green flag** and use the arrow keys to drive around.

15 Select the sprite

We need to add more code to the car, so click on the **Button 3** sprite button to select it.

16 Back to the code

Click the **Code** tab.

SENSING COLOURS

We need to set the exact shade of green for the code to work here.

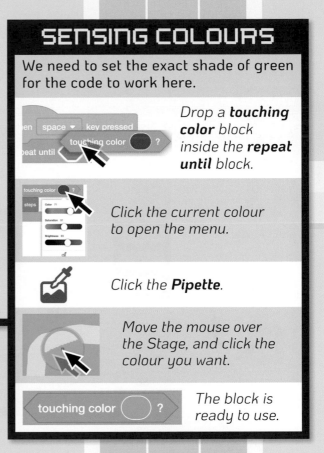

*Drop a **touching color** block inside the **repeat until** block.*

Click the current colour to open the menu.

*Click the **Pipette**.*

Move the mouse over the Stage, and click the colour you want.

The block is ready to use.

17 Fix your code

Edit your code so that the loop repeats until the car hits the green grass.

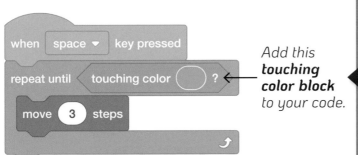

*Add this **touching color block** to your code.*

18 Test your code

Drag the car onto the track.

Make sure it is not touching any green or it won't start!

Click the **green flag** and use the arrow keys to drive around. The car should stop when it hits the green grass around the edge of the track.

If the car is stuck in the grass, drag it back on the track with your mouse.

If your car hits the green it will stop. Steer away with the arrow keys, then press the Space bar to keep driving!

19 Get the car image

We are going to make it look like a car!

Click the **Costumes** tab (on the left-hand side of the screen).

Click on **Convert to Bitmap**. This will give us simpler tools to use.

20 Zoom in!

Click the **Zoom in** button a few times. This will make it easier to add details.

21 Improve the car

Go through each of these steps to improve your car. Feel free to experiment!

Use the Undo button if you go wrong!

Rectangle

| 0 |
| 0 |
| 0 |

Use the **Rectangle** tool to draw the windows of the car.

Rectangle

| 58 |
| 1 |
| 82 |

Draw the top of the roof with another rectangle in the middle of the black rectangle.

Line

Set the thickness to 10.

| 58 |
| 1 |
| 82 |

Use the **Line** tool to draw the pillars holding the roof on top of the car.

Brush

17	0
100	100
100	100

With the **Brush** tool, add some yellow lights at the front of the car, and red ones at the rear.

Choose the tools you need and pick colours you like.

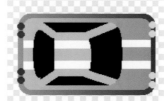

Add any other details you like!

Click the **green flag** to test your code. Now, use the arrow keys to make the car turn left or right.

Press the **Space bar** and practise driving around!

Challenges

- Make changes to the track (click the **Stage** icon, then click **Backdrops**).
- Click on the car sprite and change what it looks like.
- How can you make the car go faster? You might need to change the amount it turns when the arrow keys are used to steer it.
- Try making the car slightly smaller. How does this change the game?
- Add some extra tracks by adding another painted backdrop.
- Add some extra hazards on the track for the car to avoid.

FILLING SHAPES AND COLOUR GRADIENTS

The **Fill** tool is a great way to recolour parts of an image on a computer.

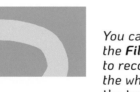

You can use the **Fill** tool to recolour the whole of the track in one click.

But some things can't be recoloured so easily.

If you try to recolour the silver car sprite it won't work properly. Only a small part of the car gets changed. Why?

The image is made up of tiny squares called **pixels**. The grey colour has been made with a gradient, so each group of pixels is a slightly different shade of grey.

The **Fill** tool will only colour in pixels that are **exactly** the same colour.

You can work round this by drawing coloured rectangles over the top of the car.

Later on in the book you'll learn lots of ways to draw your own cars!

On page 66 you'll find how to draw with gradients.

13

Two-player Race!

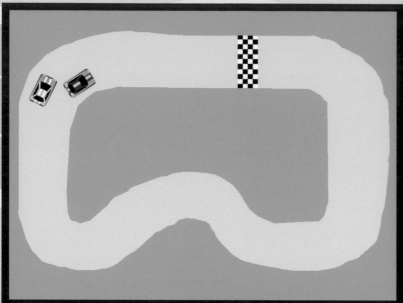

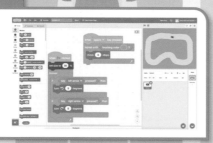

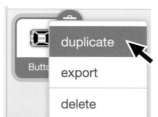

You need to have coded Track Driver before you start this project.

This is a short but exciting project! We will adapt Track Driver from page 8 to make it into a two-player game.

We will do this by duplicating the main car sprite, then setting new keys to control the second car.

Then it's time to race a friend! Who's going to win the race?

1 Start Scratch

You need to have a working copy of **Track Driver** loaded in Scratch.

If you haven't saved your Track Driver game yet then save it before you start.

2 Another car!

Right-click the **Button 3** sprite.

Button3

duplicate
export
delete

Choose **duplicate** to add another car.

Button

Duplicating also copies all the code a sprite has.

You don't need to add any code in this activity.

But you need to edit the code on the new car to change the keys used.

3 Change the code

Click the **Code** tab.

Code

14

4 Change the move key

Change **when space key pressed** to **when W key pressed**.

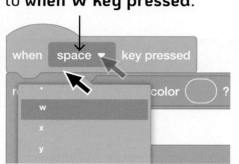

5 Change the steering keys

Just change the keys used to steer the car.

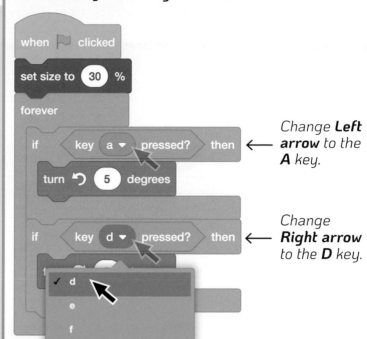

*Change **Left arrow** to the **A** key.*

*Change **Right arrow** to the **D** key.*

6 Click Costumes

Click the **Costumes** tab.

7 Respray!

Now, it's time to give the new car a new look!

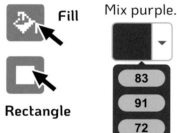 Fill

Rectangle

Mix purple.

83
91
72

Recolour parts of the car with the **Fill** and **Rectangle** tools.

Use your imagination and experiment with colours!

8 Race a friend!

 Click the **green flag**. Move the cars to the start with the mouse. Make sure they are not touching any green. Get ready — go!

 Drive

Steer

 Drive

W

Steer

A D

Challenges

- Experiment with the best keys to use.
- Make the track a bit wider so there is room for two cars.
- Add a start line to the track.
- Make a three-player version! Which keys will you use?
- Make a countdown for the start using the **say for 2 seconds** blocks.

Street Racer

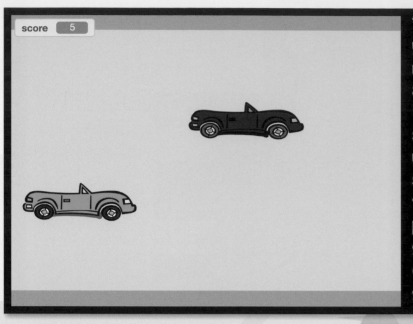

score 5

This simple game will show you how to make a sprite move up and down when keys are pressed. You will also learn how to make a second sprite move across the screen using random positioning. A score variable will be used to keep track of the players' progress, and to make the car get faster as the game goes on. If the cars crash then the game is over!

1 Start Scratch

Visit the Scratch website and create a new file.

 **scratch.mit.edu**

2 No cats

We won't need a cat. Click on the bin to delete it.

Sprite1

3 Prepare the background

Start by getting the background ready.

 **Backdrops**

Click the **Backdrops** tab.

Convert to Bitmap

Click on **Convert to Bitmap**.

4 Dark grey

Make the whole of the backdrop dark grey.

Click the **Fill** tool.

Mix dark grey.

0
0
56

Click to fill it in.

5 Draw the street

Draw a large rectangle to make the street.

Click the **Rectangle** tool.

0
0
89

Make grey.

Drag out a rectangle the width of the Stage, and almost as high.

Click Undo if things go wrong!

6 New sprite

We need a replacement for the cat, so click **Choose a Sprite**.

It's in the bottom right of the screen.

7 Find a car

Scroll through the sprites and click on **Convertible 2**.

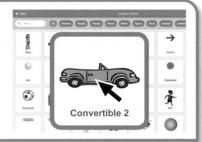

Convertible 2

8 Start coding!

Drag in these blocks to make the car move up and down when the arrow keys are pressed:

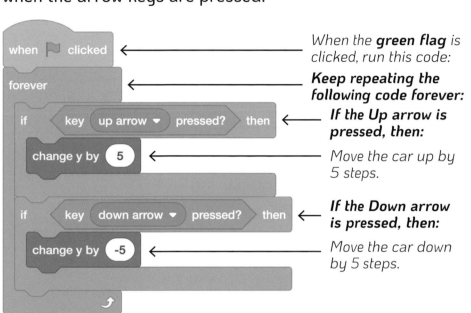

*When the **green flag** is clicked, run this code:*

Keep repeating the following code forever:

If the Up arrow is pressed, then:

Move the car up by 5 steps.

If the Down arrow is pressed, then:

Move the car down by -5 steps.

9 Test it

Click the **green flag** to test your code. Use the arrow keys to move the car up or down.

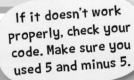

If it doesn't work properly, check your code. Make sure you used 5 and minus 5.

X AND Y COORDINATES

Sprites are positioned on the Stage by using X and Y values, called "coordinates".

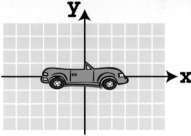

We can move a sprite left or right by changing its **x value**. Changing its **y value** will make it move up or down. We will learn more about coordinates later in the book.

10 Keeping score

We need to keep score of how many cars the player manages to overtake. We will use a **variable** to do this.

Choose the **Variables** group.

Click **Make a Variable**.

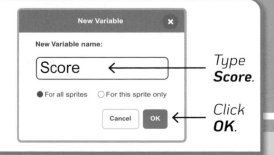

*Type **Score**.*

*Click **OK**.*

11 Bumpy roads

Add these blocks to make it look as though the car is on a bumpy road. The code will also reset the score and make sure the car is in the correct place.

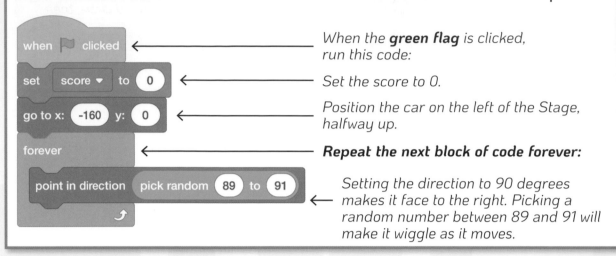

*When the **green flag** is clicked, run this code:*

Set the score to 0.

Position the car on the left of the Stage, halfway up.

Repeat the next block of code forever:

Setting the direction to 90 degrees makes it face to the right. Picking a random number between 89 and 91 will make it wiggle as it moves.

12 Rename the sprite

It will make our code clearer if we rename the sprite **player**.

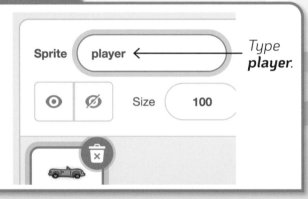

*Type **player**.*

13 Another car

We need another car to drive by, so click **Choose a Sprite**.

Random numbers are a great way to make games more varied and exciting!

USING THE PICK RANDOM BLOCK

This block is used to give other blocks a random number.

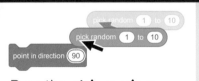

*Drag the **pick random** block over a block you want to randomise.*

Drop it in place.

Choose the range of numbers you want.

Smallest number   Largest number

14 Find a car

Scroll down and click on **Convertible 2**.

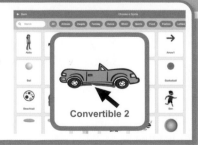

Convertible 2

Scratch shows the score automatically. But in this game we will also use the **score** variable to make the cars move faster.

*Start with a **change x by** block.*

*Drop a **minus** block inside it.*

*Type **-5** in the left-hand circle, then drop a **score** block in the right-hand circle.*

15 Code the new car

We need to make the new car start on the right-hand side and slowly move across the Stage towards the player's car. As the score goes up, the new car should go faster to make it harder.

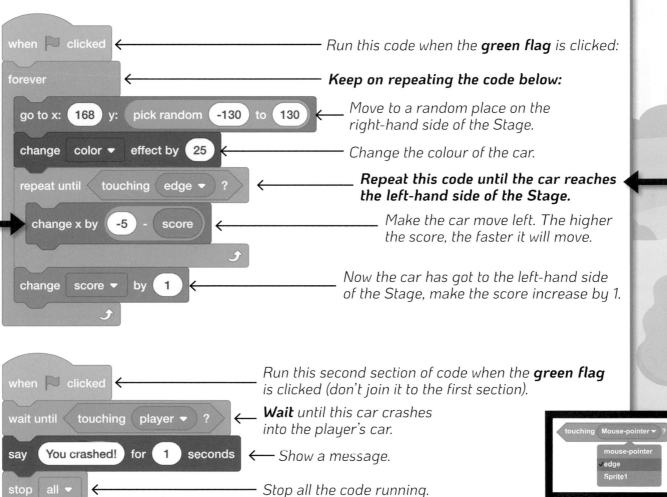

*Run this code when the **green flag** is clicked:*

Keep on repeating the code below:

Move to a random place on the right-hand side of the Stage.

Change the colour of the car.

Repeat this code until the car reaches the left-hand side of the Stage.

Make the car move left. The higher the score, the faster it will move.

Now the car has got to the left-hand side of the Stage, make the score increase by 1.

*Run this second section of code when the **green flag** is clicked (don't join it to the first section).*

***Wait** until this car crashes into the player's car.*

Show a message.

Stop all the code running.

Click the **green flag** to test your code. How many points can you score?

Challenges

- Show a different message when the game ends.
- Try using different keys to control the car.
- Change the values in the **pick random** blocks. What happens?
- Use a smaller number than 25 in the **change colour** block. What do you notice?

Snowmobile Slalom

In this two-player game, penguins race across the frozen ice avoiding ice holes. These will travel towards the penguins to make it look as though they are racing along. If the penguins hit a hole, they get pushed back towards the start. A speed variable will be used to store how fast each ice hole moves. We will use a new technique to give each hole its own speed variable.

1 Start Scratch

Visit the Scratch website and create a new file.

C **scratch.mit.edu**

2 Too cool for cats!

Click on the bin to delete the cat sprite.

3 Prepare the background

We need to get the background ready for our game.

Click the **Stage** icon.

Click the **Backdrops** tab.

Click on **Convert to Bitmap**.

If you make a mistake, click Undo!

4 Draw some ice

Add some icy water at the top of the Stage.

Choose the **Line** tool.

Mix a light blue.

54
24
100

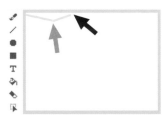

Start by drawing a series of spiky lines along the top. Don't leave gaps!

5 More ice

Add more ice at the bottom.

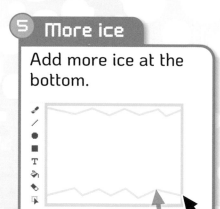

6 Fill it in

Fill in the ice.

Pick the **Fill** tool.

7 Add a painted sprite

This sprite will be some moving ice for the penguins to avoid.

Hover

Move your mouse to *hover* over the **Choose a Sprite** button.

Don't click it!

Paint

A menu like this will appear.

Move your mouse up to the **Paint** option and click it.

8 Bitmap

Click the **Convert to Bitmap** button.

If you make a mistake, click Undo!

9 Draw the ice

Now, draw an ice hole using the **Line** tool.

Choose the **Line** tool.

Mix a light blue.

54
24
100

Pick the **Fill** tool.

Make sure all the lines join up and there are no gaps!

10 Start coding

Click the **Code** tab.

21

11 How fast?

Each ice hole will move at a different random speed. We will make a special variable to do this.

Choose the **Variables** group.

Click **Make a Variable**.

New Variable

New Variable name:

speed ←

○ For all sprites ● For this sprite only ←

Cancel   OK

↑
Click OK.

Type ***speed***.

*Pick **For this sprite only**.*

This option means we can have multiple ice holes moving at different speeds.

12 Get moving

Add this code to make the ice hole move across the Stage:

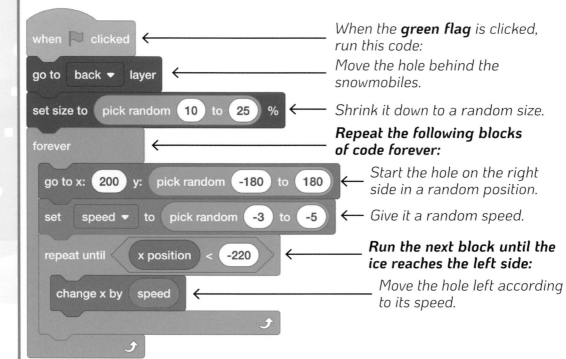

when ⚑ clicked ←

*When the **green flag** is clicked, run this code:*

go to back ▾ layer ←

Move the hole behind the snowmobiles.

set size to pick random 10 to 25 % ←

Shrink it down to a random size.

forever ←

Repeat the following blocks of code forever:

go to x: 200 y: pick random -180 to 180 ←

Start the hole on the right side in a random position.

set speed ▾ to pick random -3 to -5 ←

Give it a random speed.

repeat until x position < -220 ←

Run the next block until the ice reaches the left side:

change x by speed ←

Move the hole left according to its speed.

⚑ Test your code. The ice hole should move across the screen, then start again at the edge.

13 Another ice hole

Right-click the **Sprite1** icon.

duplicate
export
delete

Click **duplicate** to add another hole.

⚑ Both ice holes should now start moving!

14 And another!

Repeat Step 13 to make a third ice hole.

Sprite1   Sprite2   Sprite3

Duplicating copies all the code a sprite has too.

15 Add a sprite

We need a snowmobile, so click **Choose a Sprite**.

16 Find a penguin

Scroll down the sprites and click on **Penguin 2**.

Penguin 2

17 Face sideways

The penguin needs to look where it's going!

 Costumes

Click the **Costumes** tab.

Pick the third costume, where the penguin is looking sideways.

18 Bitmap

Click the **Convert to Bitmap** button.

 Convert to Bitmap

19 Draw the snowmobile

Start by drawing the body of the snowmobile.

Choose the **Brush** tool.

Set the thickness to 30.

| 0 |
| 100 |
| 100 |

Mix a red colour.

20 Complete the snowmobile

Finish drawing the snowmobile.

Choose the **Line** tool.

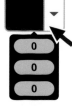

| 0 |
| 0 |
| 0 |

Pick black.

Add a track to the back.

Draw one on the front.

Add any other details you want to the snowmobile.

21 Code the snowmobile

Add this code to make the snowmobile move up and down:

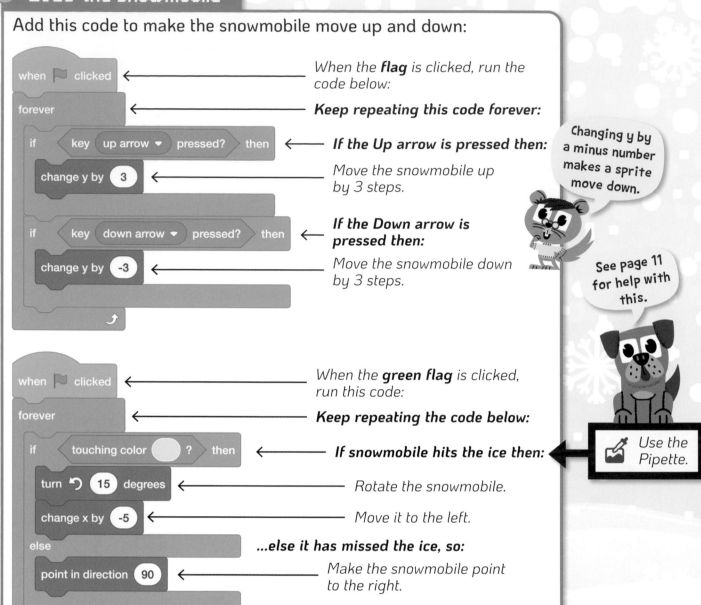

when ⚑ clicked ← *When the **flag** is clicked, run the code below:*

forever ← ***Keep repeating this code forever:***

if ⟨ key up arrow ▼ pressed? ⟩ then ← ***If the Up arrow is pressed then:***

change y by 3 ← *Move the snowmobile up by 3 steps.*

if ⟨ key down arrow ▼ pressed? ⟩ then ← ***If the Down arrow is pressed then:***

change y by -3 ← *Move the snowmobile down by 3 steps.*

Changing y by a minus number makes a sprite move down.

See page 11 for help with this.

when ⚑ clicked ← *When the **green flag** is clicked, run this code:*

forever ← ***Keep repeating the code below:***

if ⟨ touching color ⬤ ? ⟩ then ← ***If snowmobile hits the ice then:***

🖊 *Use the Pipette.*

turn ↺ 15 degrees ← *Rotate the snowmobile.*

change x by -5 ← *Move it to the left.*

else ← ***...else it has missed the ice, so:***

point in direction 90 ← *Make the snowmobile point to the right.*

⚑ Test your code.

22 Code the snowmobile

Add this code to make the snowmobile move to the right:

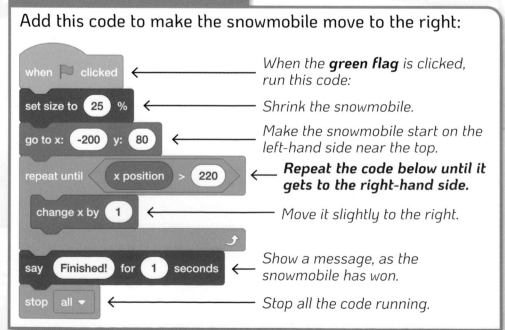

when ⚑ clicked ← *When the **green flag** is clicked, run this code:*

set size to 25 % ← *Shrink the snowmobile.*

go to x: -200 y: 80 ← *Make the snowmobile start on the left-hand side near the top.*

repeat until ⟨ x position > 220 ⟩ ← ***Repeat the code below until it gets to the right-hand side.***

change x by 1 ← *Move it slightly to the right.*

say Finished! for 1 seconds ← *Show a message, as the snowmobile has won.*

stop all ▼ ← *Stop all the code running.*

23 Another snowmobile

Right-click the **Penguin 2** sprite.

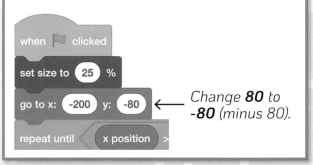

Click **duplicate** to add another snowmobile.

duplicate
export
delete

24 Change the keys

Change the keys that control the snowmobile.

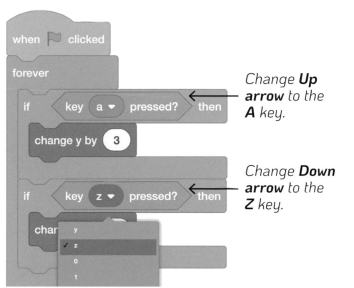

when 🏳 clicked

forever

if key a ▼ pressed? then

change y by 3

if key z ▼ pressed? then

char y
  ✓ z
    0
    1

*Change **Up arrow** to the **A** key.*

*Change **Down arrow** to the **Z** key.*

25 Change the start position

Make the second snowmobile start lower down.

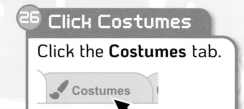

when 🏳 clicked

set size to 25 %

go to x: -200 y: -80

repeat until x position >

*Change **80** to **-80** (minus 80).*

26 Click Costumes

Click the **Costumes** tab.

Costumes

27 Respray!

Fill the snowmobile in yellow — or any other colour!

Select the **Fill** tool.

17
100
100

Pick yellow.

Fill the second snowmobile in yellow.

Find a friend and race your snowmobiles!

Challenges

- Add a fourth ice hole by duplicating one of the others. Would five be too many?

- The size of each hole is between 10 and 25. Experiment with different values. You may have to change the starting x value from 200 to 170 or 180.

- Can you make the snowmobiles faster? Does that make the game too easy?

- Try to add some sound effects.

Big Track Racer

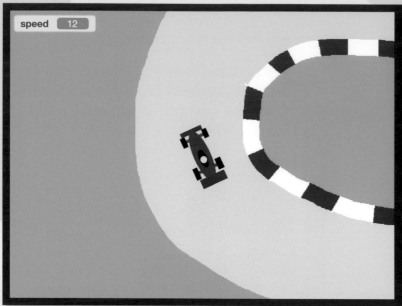

speed 12

The first games in this book showed the whole of the race track on the screen. This meant the car had to be quite small to fit it. In this game you will learn how to code a game where a much larger track is used. Instead of the car moving, the track will move around! We will create a very large sprite to be the track, and move it in the opposite direction to where the car is pointing.

1 Start Scratch

Visit the Scratch website and create a new file.

↻ scratch.mit.edu

2 No cats

We won't need a cat. Click on the bin to delete it.

Sprite1

3 How fast?

We need to know how fast the car is going, so create a variable called **speed**.

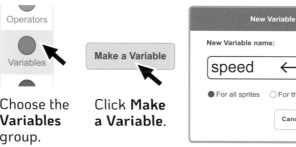

Operators

Variables

Choose the **Variables** group.

Make a Variable

Click **Make a Variable**.

New Variable ✕

New Variable name:

speed ←

● For all sprites ○ For this sprite only

Cancel **OK** ←

Type speed.

Click OK.

4 Add a painted sprite

This sprite will be the racing car.

Hover

Move your mouse to **hover** over the **Choose a Sprite** button.

Don't click it!

Paint

A menu like this will appear.

Move your mouse up to the **Paint** option and click it.

5 Bitmap

Click the **Convert to Bitmap** button.

🖼 Convert to Bitmap

Use the Undo button if your picture goes wrong.

6 Draw a racing car

Go through these steps to draw the racing car:

Rectangle

Use the **Rectangle** tool to draw the two car axles.

Rectangle

Add a dark red front wing to the car.

Oval

Draw a lighter red oval to be the body of the car.

Oval

Draw the cockpit in black.

  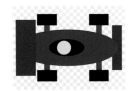

Oval

Put the driver in the car.

Rectangle

Add the tyres with four black rectangles.

  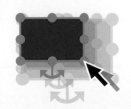

Rectangle

Use dark red to add the rear wing.

Add any other details you want.

If you don't fix a shape in place it may change colour when you start the next shape.

DRAWING TIPS

Once you have drawn a shape in Scratch you can still make changes to it.

Use the handles to resize or rotate the shape.

Drag the middle of the shape to move it.

You can also use the arrow keys to *nudge* it.

To fix the shape in place, click anywhere outside the shape.

Use the **Undo** button if you need to try again.

27

7 Code the steering

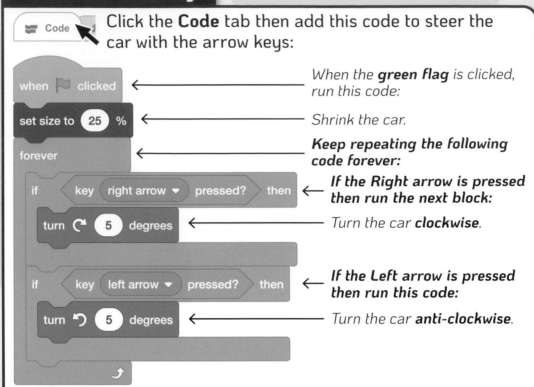

Code Click the **Code** tab then add this code to steer the car with the arrow keys:

when 🏳 clicked ← *When the **green flag** is clicked, run this code:*

set size to 25 % ← *Shrink the car.*

forever ← ***Keep repeating the following code forever:***

if `key right arrow pressed?` then ← ***If the Right arrow is pressed then run the next block:***

turn ↻ 5 degrees ← *Turn the car **clockwise**.*

if `key left arrow pressed?` then ← ***If the Left arrow is pressed then run this code:***

turn ↺ 5 degrees ← *Turn the car **anti-clockwise**.*

8 Accelerate and brake

This code will speed up and slow down the car a small amount.

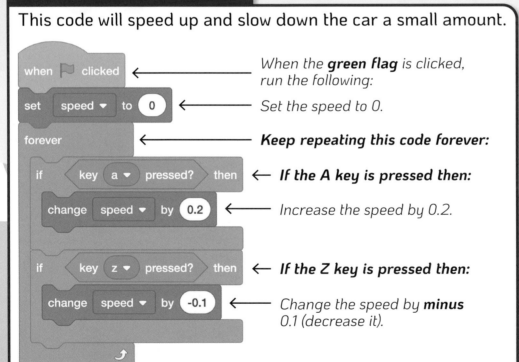

when 🏳 clicked ← *When the **green flag** is clicked, run the following:*

set speed to 0 ← *Set the speed to 0.*

forever ← ***Keep repeating this code forever:***

if `key a pressed?` then ← ***If the A key is pressed then:***

change speed by 0.2 ← *Increase the speed by 0.2.*

if `key z pressed?` then ← ***If the Z key is pressed then:***

change speed by -0.1 ← *Change the speed by **minus 0.1** (decrease it).*

> An extension adds some extra code blocks to allow you to do more things with Scratch.

9 Import the Music extension

We need to create some sound that changes its pitch, so we will add an **extension** to Scratch.

 Click the **Add Extension** button.

 Choose the **Music** extension.

10 Add the engine sound

This code will create an engine noise by using a clarinet sound!

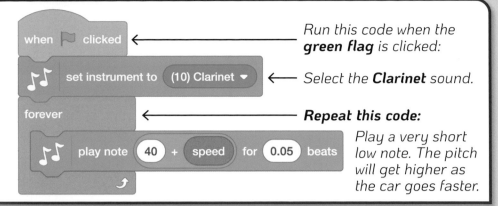

*Run this code when the **green flag** is clicked:*

*Select the **Clarinet** sound.*

Repeat this code:

Play a very short low note. The pitch will get higher as the car goes faster.

11 Add a sprite

We will use this sprite to be the track.

Move your mouse to *hover* over the **Choose a Sprite** button.

Click the **Paint** option.

Normally, you might draw the track on the background, but our track will scroll around.

So, it needs to be a sprite!

Our sprite needs two costumes.

12 Add an extra costume

This will help us make the track big enough.

Hover over the **Choose a Costume** button in the bottom-left corner.

The menu will show.

Move the mouse to the **Paint** option and click it.

CHOOSE A SPRITE OR CHOOSE A COSTUME?

Careful! These buttons look the same but do different things!

Choose a **Costume**.   Choose a **Sprite**.

A **sprite** can move around and have code of its own.

A **costume** is a picture that is shown on a sprite. A sprite can have many different costumes — just like a person!

13 Bitmap

Click **Convert to Bitmap**.

14 Green grass

Make the whole of the sprite costume green.

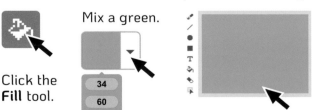

Mix a green.

Click the **Fill** tool.

34
60
78

Fill the sprite in green.

Your Costumes panel should now look like this:

15 Ready to draw

Get ready to draw the track.

 Choose the **Brush** tool.

Mix light grey.

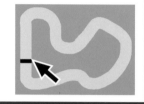

0
0
89

Set the brush thickness to 90.

90 ⬍

If you make a mistake, click Undo.

16 Draw the track

Draw the track carefully. Choose the shape you want it to be.

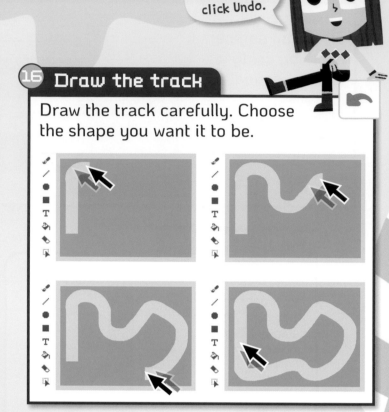

17 Add the start line

Draw the start line in black.

Rectangle

0
0
0

18 Code tab

☰ Code

Select the **Code** tab.

19 Code the track

In this game, instead of moving the car forward, we will move the track backwards.

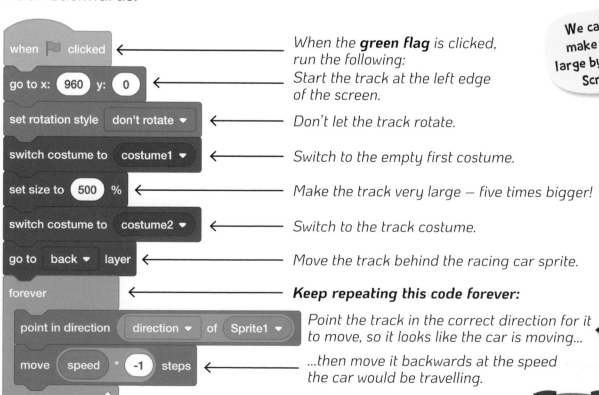

when 🏳 clicked ⟵ *When the **green flag** is clicked, run the following:*

go to x: 960 y: 0 ⟵ *Start the track at the left edge of the screen.*

set rotation style don't rotate ▾ ⟵ *Don't let the track rotate.*

switch costume to costume1 ▾ ⟵ *Switch to the empty first costume.*

set size to 500 % ⟵ *Make the track very large – five times bigger!*

switch costume to costume2 ▾ ⟵ *Switch to the track costume.*

go to back ▾ layer ⟵ *Move the track behind the racing car sprite.*

forever ⟵ ***Keep repeating this code forever:***

point in direction direction ▾ of Sprite1 ▾ *Point the track in the correct direction for it to move, so it looks like the car is moving...*

move speed * -1 steps ⟵ *...then move it backwards at the speed the car would be travelling.*

We can only make it this large by tricking Scratch!

So we pick an empty costume (costume1) before setting the size...

...then we switch to the costume we want.

30

Test the game

Click the **green flag**. Press the
A key to start moving, and use
the arrow keys to steer the car.

A	Accelerate	Steer
Z	Brake	← →

Check for crashes

Finally, we need to stop the car if it goes off the track. Add this code:

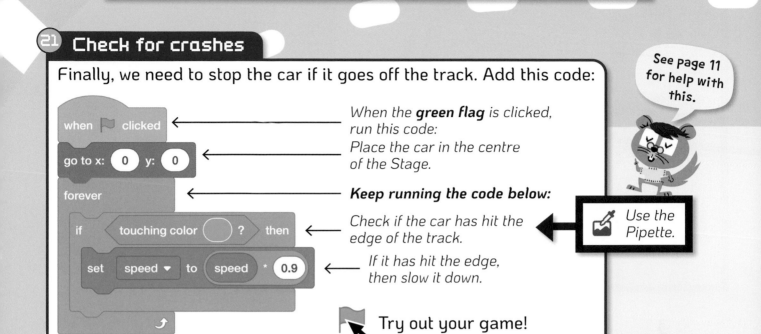

*When the **green flag** is clicked,
run this code:*
*Place the car in the centre
of the Stage.*

Keep running the code below:

*Check if the car has hit the
edge of the track.*

*If it has hit the edge,
then slow it down.*

See page 11 for help with this.

Use the Pipette.

Try out your game!

Challenges

- Change what your car looks like. You could even upload a photo.

- The car turns 5 degrees when you use the arrow keys. Try using other numbers. How does this affect the game?

- Click **Choose a Costume** again (see Step 12) and make a different track. Change the code in Step 19 to show the new track when the code runs.

- Experiment with the way the engine sound is made. Are other instruments more effective? Try using different values from 40 and 0.05 in the **play note** box.

*Drop a **backdrop# of Stage** block
inside a **point in direction** block.*

*Set this drop-
down to **Sprite1**.*

*Pick
direction.*

Desert Drifter

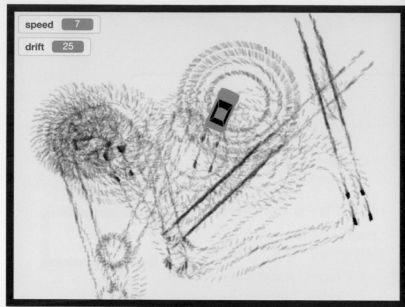

This game allows the player to drift (skid or slide) a car around the screen. The cat will drive around using similar code to the Track Driver game, but will be invisible. We will place a visible car on top of it, but make it turn more than the hidden cat so it looks like it is drifting. The pen code blocks will be used to make tyre marks as it drives.

1 Start Scratch

Visit the Scratch website and create a new file.

scratch.mit.edu

2 The speed

We need to know how fast the car is going, so create a variable called **speed**.

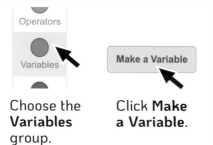

Choose the **Variables** group.

Click **Make a Variable**.

New Variable

New Variable name:

| speed |

● For all sprites ○ For this sprite only

Cancel OK

Type ***speed***.

Click ***OK***.

3 The drift

The car is going to drift (skid) as it goes round a corner. We need to store how much it is drifting by.

Make a Variable

Click **Make a Variable**.

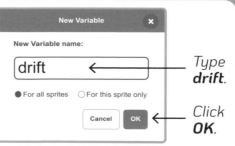

New Variable

New Variable name:

| drift |

● For all sprites ○ For this sprite only

Cancel OK

Type ***drift***.

Click ***OK***.

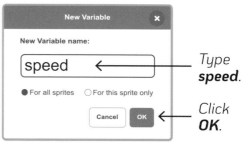

4 Start coding!

Drag in these code blocks. They will start the invisible cat driving around.

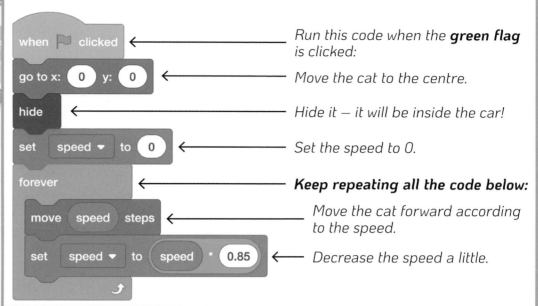

*Run this code when the **green flag** is clicked:*

Move the cat to the centre.

Hide it — it will be inside the car!

Set the speed to 0.

Keep repeating all the code below:

Move the cat forward according to the speed.

Decrease the speed a little.

5 Add a painted sprite

Add a sprite to use as the car.

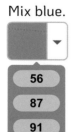

Hover

Move your mouse to **hover** over the **Choose a Sprite** button.

Don't click it!

Paint

A menu like this will appear.

Move your mouse up to the **Paint** option and click it.

6 Bitmap

Click the **Convert to Bitmap** button.

Convert to Bitmap

7 Outline the car

Just draw a very large rectangle to outline the car. We'll add details later. Our code will shrink it down.

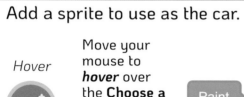

Mix blue.

56
87
91

Select the **Rectangle** tool.

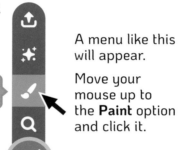

IN THE CENTRE

The rectangle needs to be exactly in the centre of the drawing area.

Hold the mouse button down and move the rectangle towards the centre.

Aim for the target in the centre and it will snap into place. Release the mouse button.

Make sure it is in the centre of the drawing area.

8 Rename the sprite

Our code will be clearer if we rename the sprite **car**.

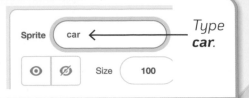

Sprite **car** ← *Type car.*

Size 100

9 More code

Click the **Code** tab.

Code

10 Move the car to the cat

The actual car needs to move to the cat, and point at the correct angle.

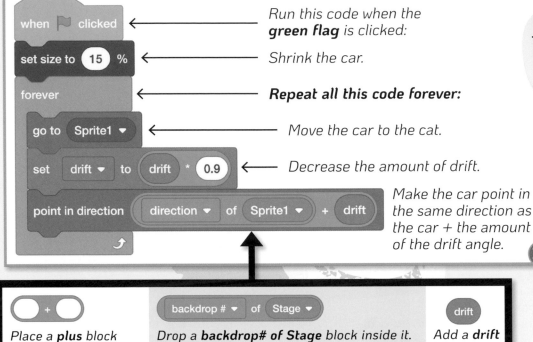

when ⚑ clicked ← *Run this code when the **green flag** is clicked:*

set size to **15** % ← *Shrink the car.*

forever ← **Repeat all this code forever:**

go to **Sprite1 ▾** ← *Move the car to the cat.*

set **drift ▾** to (**drift** * **0.9**) ← *Decrease the amount of drift.*

point in direction (**direction ▾** of **Sprite1 ▾** + **drift**)

Make the car point in the same direction as the car + the amount of the drift angle.

Next, we need to add more code to the cat sprite. Make sure you select it first.

(◯ **+** ◯)

*Place a **plus** block inside the **point** block.*

(**backdrop # ▾** of **Stage ▾**)

*Drop a **backdrop# of Stage** block inside it. Change Stage to Sprite1, then pick direction.*

(**drift**)

*Add a **drift** block.*

11 Select the cat

Click the cat sprite.

Sprite1   car

12 Forward and reverse

Add this code to the **cat sprite** to make it move forwards and backwards:

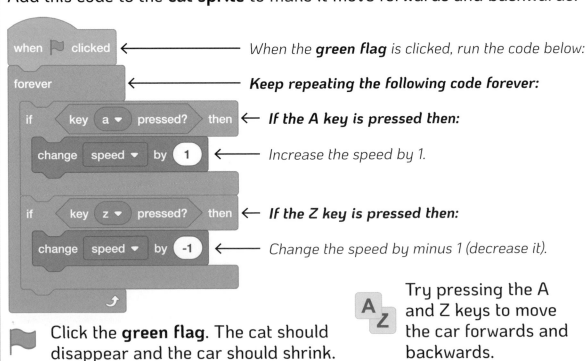

when ⚑ clicked ← *When the **green flag** is clicked, run the code below:*

forever ← **Keep repeating the following code forever:**

if ⟨ key **a ▾** pressed? ⟩ then ← **If the A key is pressed then:**

change **speed ▾** by **1** ← *Increase the speed by 1.*

if ⟨ key **z ▾** pressed? ⟩ then ← **If the Z key is pressed then:**

change **speed ▾** by **-1** ← *Change the speed by minus 1 (decrease it).*

⚑ Click the **green flag**. The cat should disappear and the car should shrink.

A Z Try pressing the A and Z keys to move the car forwards and backwards.

13 Left and right

Now, add these blocks to steer left and right:

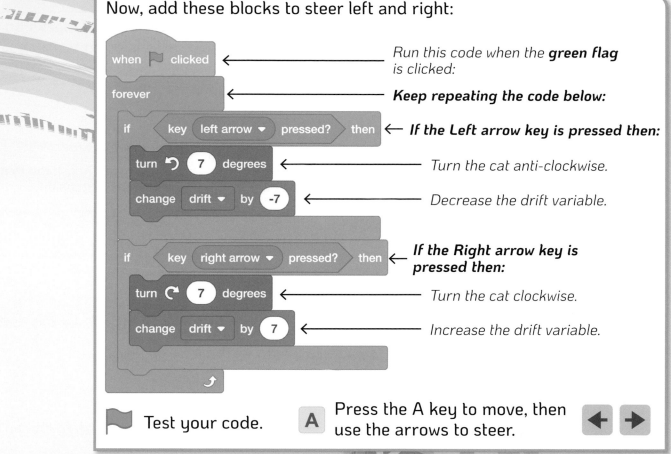

when 🏳 clicked ← *Run this code when the **green flag** is clicked:*

forever ← ***Keep repeating the code below:***

if key left arrow pressed? then ← ***If the Left arrow key is pressed then:***

turn ↺ 7 degrees ← *Turn the cat anti-clockwise.*

change drift by -7 ← *Decrease the drift variable.*

if key right arrow pressed? then ← ***If the Right arrow key is pressed then:***

turn ↻ 7 degrees ← *Turn the cat clockwise.*

change drift by 7 ← *Increase the drift variable.*

🏳 Test your code.

A Press the A key to move, then use the arrows to steer.

← →

14 Add another painted sprite

This sprite will make skid marks as the car moves.

Hover Move your mouse to ***hover*** over the **Choose a Sprite** button.

Don't click it!

A menu like this will appear.

Paint

Move your mouse up to the **Paint** option and click it.

15 Bitmap

Click the **Convert to Bitmap** button.

🖼 Convert to Bitmap

16 Draw the skid marks

Use the **Brush** tool to draw four rough black marks where the tyres of the car would be. Spread them out like this:

Select the **Brush** tool.

Mix black.

0
0
0

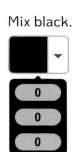

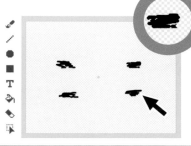

They don't need to be neat – just a small scribble!

17 Back to coding

Click the **Code** tab.

---

backdrop # ▼ of Stage ▼

*Drop a **backdrop# of Stage** block inside the **point in direction** block. Change Stage to Sprite4, then pick direction.*

---

18 Import the drawing blocks

We need some extra blocks to draw the skid marks on the backdrop, so we will add an extension to Scratch.

Click the **Add Extension** button (in the bottom left of the screen).

Choose the **Pen** extension.

---

19 Code the skid marks

Add this code to make the marks appear when the car moves:

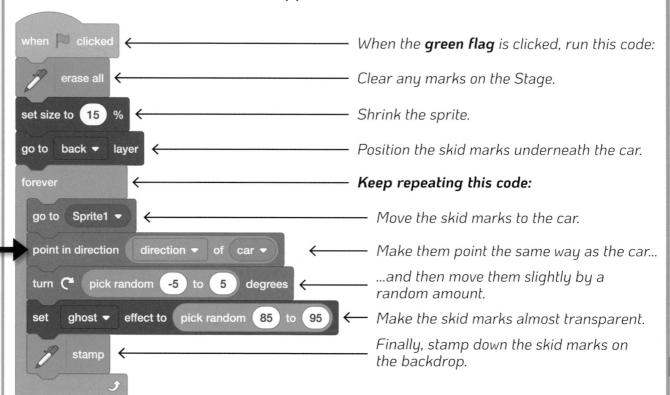

when 🏳 clicked ←——————— *When the **green flag** is clicked, run this code:*

🖊 erase all ←——————— *Clear any marks on the Stage.*

set size to 15 % ←——————— *Shrink the sprite.*

go to back ▼ layer ←——————— *Position the skid marks underneath the car.*

forever ←——————— ***Keep repeating this code:***

  go to Sprite1 ▼ ←——————— *Move the skid marks to the car.*

  point in direction direction ▼ of car ▼ ←——————— *Make them point the same way as the car...*

  turn ↻ pick random -5 to 5 degrees ←——————— *...and then move them slightly by a random amount.*

  set ghost ▼ effect to pick random 85 to 95 ←——————— *Make the skid marks almost transparent.*

  🖊 stamp ←——————— *Finally, stamp down the skid marks on the backdrop.*

🏳 Test your code. Press the A key and drive around with the arrow keys!

---

20 Select the car

Click the car sprite.

---

21 Import the Music extension

We need to create some sound that changes its pitch, so we will add another extension to Scratch.

Click the **Add Extension** button.

Choose the **Music** extension.

22 Add a sound effect

This code will make the engine noise of the car as it moves.

when 🏁 clicked ← *Run this code when the **green flag** is clicked:*

♪ set instrument to (1) Piano ▼ ← *Select the **Piano** sound.*

forever ← ***Repeat this code:***

♪ play note speed for 0.1 beats ← *Play a short low note. The pitch will get slightly higher as the car goes faster.*

🏁 Test your code!

We need to finish drawing the car!

23 Click Costumes

Click the **Costumes** tab.

🖌 Costumes

If you make a mistake, click Undo!

24 Finish the car

Finally, we will complete drawing the car.

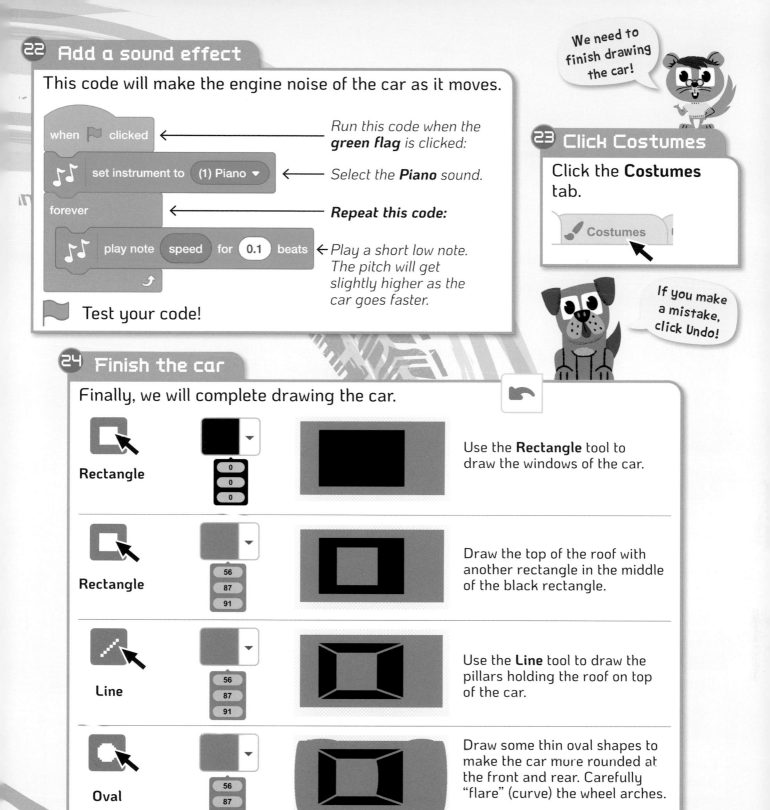

Rectangle	0 / 0 / 0		Use the **Rectangle** tool to draw the windows of the car.
Rectangle	56 / 87 / 91		Draw the top of the roof with another rectangle in the middle of the black rectangle.
Line	56 / 87 / 91		Use the **Line** tool to draw the pillars holding the roof on top of the car.
Oval	56 / 87 / 91		Draw some thin oval shapes to make the car more rounded at the front and rear. Carefully "flare" (curve) the wheel arches. Add any other details you like!

Challenges

- Draw a background on the Stage. It could just be a plain sandy yellow colour or you could add some roads.
- Experiment with the amount turned, and the amount the drift variable is changed (in Step 13).
- Can you make the car go faster?
- Try using different instruments to make the car engine noise.

Formula Racer

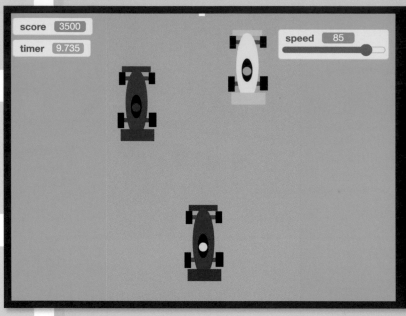

score 3500
timer 9.735
speed 85

Formula Racer gives players the chance to race against computer-driven cars. A coding technique called "cloning" will create a copy of a racing car every second. These cars will move down the screen towards the player. Variables will be used to store how fast the cars are going, and the total score. If the player hits one of the cars, the speed will drop.

1 Start Scratch

Visit the Scratch website and create a new file.

↻ **scratch.mit.edu**

2 No cats

We won't need a cat. Click on the bin to delete it.

Sprite1

3 Prepare the background

Start by getting the background ready.

 **Backdrops**

 Convert to Bitmap

Click the **Backdrops** tab.

Click on **Convert to Bitmap**.

4 Green grass

Make the whole of the backdrop green.

Click the **Fill** tool.

Mix a green.

34
60
78

Fill it with green.

5 Grey track

Draw a simple rectangle to make the track.

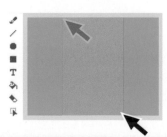

Click the **Rectangle** tool.

0
0
89

Mix grey.

Drag out a rectangle about half the width of the drawing area to be the track.

If you make a mistake, click Undo!

6 Add a painted sprite

Add a sprite to use as the car.

Hover

Hover over the **Choose a Sprite** button.
Don't click it!

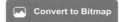

A menu will show.

Move up to the **Paint** option and click it.

7 Bitmap

Click the **Convert to Bitmap** button.

8 Racing car

Draw a racing car.

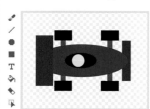

Turn back to page 27 for detailed instructions!

9 Shrink it

Size   5

Get the car out of the way for now. Set the size to 5. Our code will make it bigger later on.

10 Start coding

Code

Click the **Code** tab.

11 Speed

Create a variable called **speed** to store how fast the car is moving.

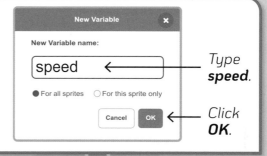

Choose the **Variables** group.

Click **Make a Variable**.

Type ***speed***.

Click ***OK***.

12 Score

Make another variable to keep the score.

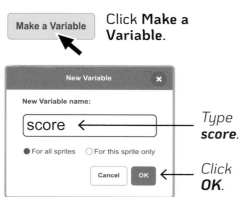

Click **Make a Variable**.

Type ***score***.

Click ***OK***.

13 Another car

Right-click the **Sprite1** icon.

Click **duplicate** to add another car.

We will use code to make more copies of this second car. This is called "cloning"!

14 Lots of cars!

This code will create another copy of the car every second!

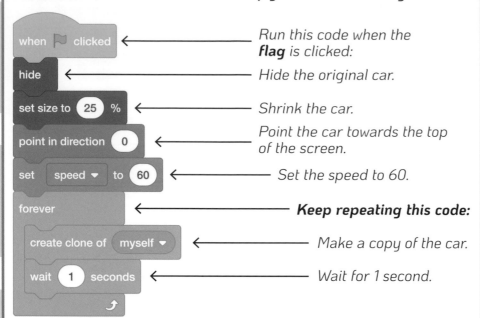

```
when 🏳 clicked
hide
set size to 25 %
point in direction 0
set speed ▾ to 60
forever
    create clone of myself ▾
    wait 1 seconds
```

Run this code when the **flag** is clicked:

Hide the original car.

Shrink the car.

Point the car towards the top of the screen.

Set the speed to 60.

Keep repeating this code:

Make a copy of the car.

Wait for 1 second.

15 Make them move

After each clone is created, this code will randomise it and make it move down the screen.

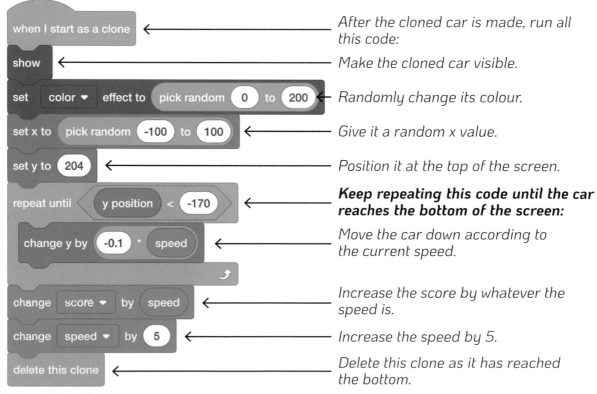

```
when I start as a clone
show
set color ▾ effect to pick random 0 to 200
set x to pick random -100 to 100
set y to 204
repeat until y position < -170
    change y by -0.1 * speed
change score ▾ by speed
change speed ▾ by 5
delete this clone
```

After the cloned car is made, run all this code:

Make the cloned car visible.

Randomly change its colour.

Give it a random x value.

Position it at the top of the screen.

Keep repeating this code until the car reaches the bottom of the screen:

Move the car down according to the current speed.

Increase the score by whatever the speed is.

Increase the speed by 5.

Delete this clone as it has reached the bottom.

🏳 Try out your code. Different coloured cars should start moving down the screen.

Who are you?

I'm a clone.

Me too!

16 Import an extension

We need to play a drum sound when the cars collide, so we will add an extension to Scratch.

Click the **Add Extension** button.

Choose the **Music** extension.

17 Check for collisions

Each cloned car needs to check if it has hit the player's car — Sprite1.

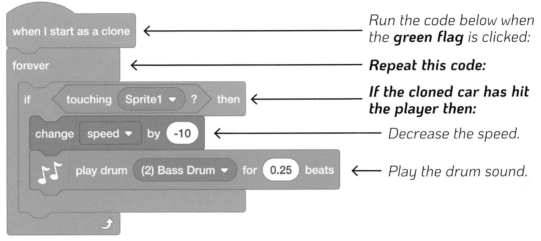

*Run the code below when the **green flag** is clicked:*

Repeat this code:

If the cloned car has hit the player then:

Decrease the speed.

Play the drum sound.

🏁 Test the code. Every time the cars collide, a drum will sound and they will all slow down.

18 Select the first car

Click the **Sprite1** icon.

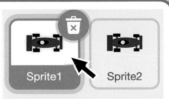

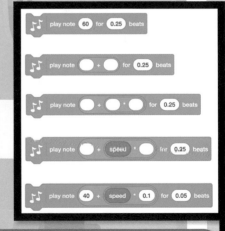

19 Add a sound effect

This code will make the engine noise of the car as it speeds up.

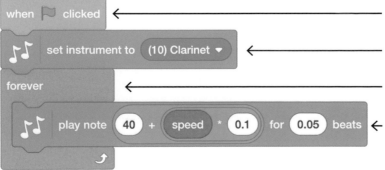

*Run this code when the **green flag** is clicked:*

*Select the **Clarinet** sound.*

Repeat this code:

← *Play a short low note. The pitch will get higher as the car goes faster.*

20 Move left and right

Add this code to steer the car left and right:

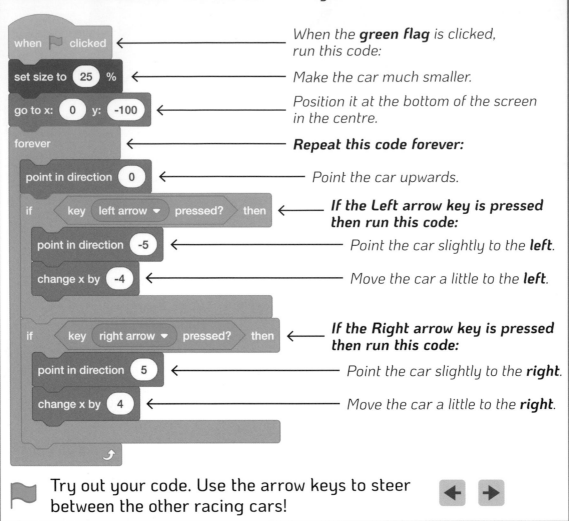

when ⚑ clicked — *When the **green flag** is clicked, run this code:*

set size to 25 % — *Make the car much smaller.*

go to x: 0 y: -100 — *Position it at the bottom of the screen in the centre.*

forever — ***Repeat this code forever:***

point in direction 0 — *Point the car upwards.*

if key left arrow pressed? then — ***If the Left arrow key is pressed then run this code:***

point in direction -5 — *Point the car slightly to the **left**.*

change x by -4 — *Move the car a little to the **left**.*

if key right arrow pressed? then — ***If the Right arrow key is pressed then run this code:***

point in direction 5 — *Point the car slightly to the **right**.*

change x by 4 — *Move the car a little to the **right**.*

⚑ Try out your code. Use the arrow keys to steer between the other racing cars!

21 Stop at zero

This code will make the game stop if the speed drops too low.

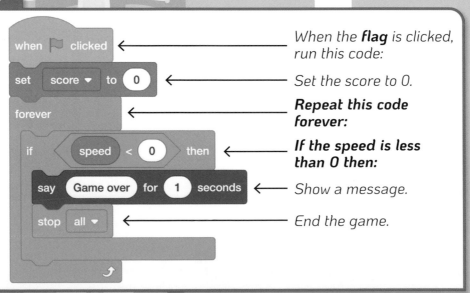

when ⚑ clicked — *When the **flag** is clicked, run this code:*

set score to 0 — *Set the score to 0.*

forever — ***Repeat this code forever:***

if speed < 0 then — ***If the speed is less than 0 then:***

say Game over for 1 seconds — *Show a message.*

stop all — *End the game.*

22 Show the timer

We want to show how long the game has been running.

Control — Sensing — Pick the **Sensing** group.

Control — Sensing — timer — Click the box next to the **timer** block.

23 Keep off the grass

Add this code to slow down the car if it hits the grass:

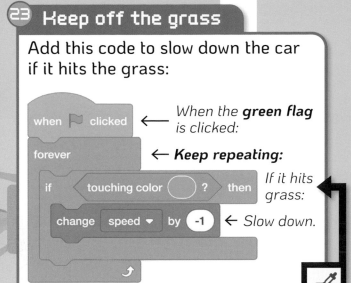

when ⚑ clicked ← *When the **green flag** is clicked:*

forever ← ***Keep repeating:***

if ⟨ touching color ◯ ? ⟩ then *If it hits grass:*

change speed ▾ by -1 ← *Slow down.*

24 Time limit!

And add this code to stop the game after 30 seconds:

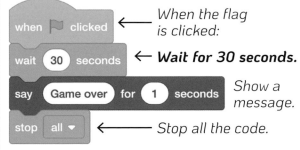

when ⚑ clicked ← *When the flag is clicked:*

wait 30 seconds ← ***Wait for 30 seconds.***

say Game over for 1 seconds *Show a message.*

stop all ▾ ← *Stop all the code.*

⚑ How many points can you score before the time runs out?

25 Add a painted sprite

This sprite will be the road markings.

Hover over the **Choose a Sprite** button.
Don't click it!

A menu will show.

Move up to the **Paint** option and click it.

26 Bitmap

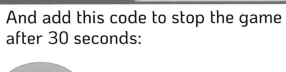

Convert to Bitmap

Click the **Convert to Bitmap** button.

27 Start drawing

This sprite will be the white line in the road.

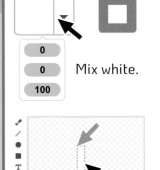

0
0
100

Mix white.

Draw a rectangle in the centre of the Stage.

28 Make it move

Code

Click the **Code** tab, then make the line move with this:

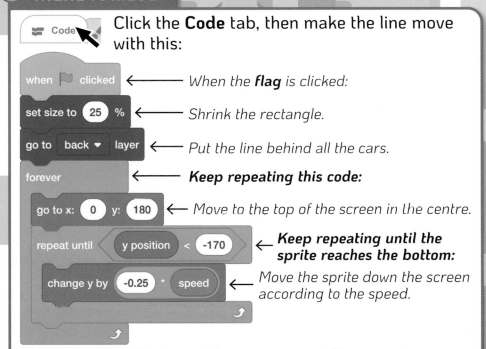

when ⚑ clicked ← *When the **flag** is clicked:*

set size to 25 % ← *Shrink the rectangle.*

go to back ▾ layer ← *Put the line behind all the cars.*

forever ← ***Keep repeating this code:***

go to x: 0 y: 180 ← *Move to the top of the screen in the centre.*

repeat until ⟨ y position < -170 ⟩ ← ***Keep repeating until the sprite reaches the bottom:***

change y by -0.25 * speed ← *Move the sprite down the screen according to the speed.*

Challenges

• Make the game last for 1 minute instead of 30 seconds.

• Change how quickly the speed increases each time a car is overtaken.

• Make a new car appear more often – every half-second.

Muturi cr uss Riue r

ySpeed 0.5
speed -0.1

Motorcross Rider lets you zoom over some pretty tricky hills! One variable will store the speed of the bike. Another will simulate gravity, making the bike drop down to the ground.

Our code will check when each wheel has touched the ground. When you speed up, code will make the bike rotate slightly, causing it to do a "wheelie" and stand on its back wheels.

HOW THE GAME WORKS

A variable called **ySpeed** will make the bike drop down if there is nothing to stop it falling.

If the front wheel hits the ground, the bike will rotate slightly clockwise. The **ySpeed** variable will be changed to make it bounce up.

If the back wheel hits the ground, the bike will rotate anti-clockwise a little. It will also bounce up.

 When the **Right** arrow key is pressed, the speed variable increases and the bike rotates anti-clockwise into a wheelie on the back wheel.

When the **Left** arrow key is pressed, the speed variable decreases and the bike rotates.

44

1 Start Scratch

Visit the Scratch website and create a new file.

scratch.mit.edu

2 No cats

We don't need the cat, so click on the bin to delete it.

Sprite1

3 How fast?

Our first variable is going to store how fast the bike is going across the ground. Create a variable called **speed**.

Operators

Variables

Choose the **Variables** group.

Make a Variable

Click **Make a Variable**.

New Variable

New Variable name:

speed ←

● For all sprites   ○ For this sprite only

Cancel   OK

*Type **speed**.*

*Click **OK**.*

4 Gravity

We also need a variable to simulate gravity and make the bike move downwards. We will call this variable **ySpeed**.

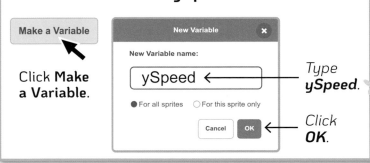

Make a Variable

Click **Make a Variable**.

New Variable

New Variable name:

ySpeed ←

● For all sprites   ○ For this sprite only

Cancel   OK

*Type **ySpeed**.*

*Click **OK**.*

This will store how fast the bike is going up or down.

5 Add a sprite

This will become the motorbike.

Move your mouse to *hover* over the **Choose a Sprite** button.

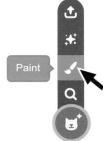

Paint

A menu will appear.

Move your mouse up to the **Paint** option and click it.

6 Bitmap

Convert to Bitmap

Click the **Convert to Bitmap** button.

Stick to these colours for now. If you change some of them, the code won't work.

7 Start drawing the motorbike

Follow these steps carefully to draw the motorbike.

 Oval

 Filled Outlined Thickness **25**

Click the **Oval** tool. Choose **Outlined** and set the thickness to 25. Hold down the **Shift** key while you draw the back wheel.

Oval

| 0 |
| 0 |
| 56 |

Draw a lighter grey wheel to be the front wheel.

Line

| 0 |
| 100 |
| 100 |

Add the front forks with a thick red line.

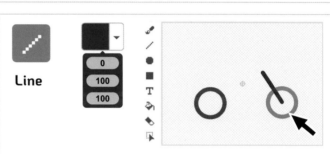

Line

| 0 |
| 100 |
| 100 |

Draw the rear "swing arm" that connects the wheel.

Click Undo if you make a mistake.

Line

| 0 |
| 100 |
| 100 |

Draw more red lines to finish off the body of the bike.

8 Finish the motorbike

Fill

Fill in the body of the motorbike.

Line

Start drawing the rider's legs.

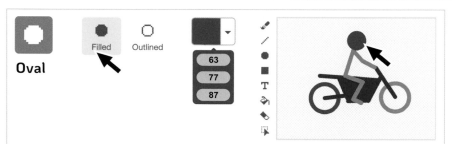

Use blue lines to finish the legs. Add the body and arms.

Oval

Filled   Outlined

63
77
87

Set the oval to **Filled** then draw the driver's helmet in darker blue.

Add any other details you want!

Remember, the wheels need to be different colours!

9 Start coding!

Click the **Code** tab.

 Code

10 Import the Music extension

To make the engine sound realistic, we need to be able to change its pitch. So, add the **Music** extension to Scratch.

Click the **Add Extension** button.

Choose the **Music** extension.

11 Add the engine sound effect

The motorbike engine sound will be made by this code.

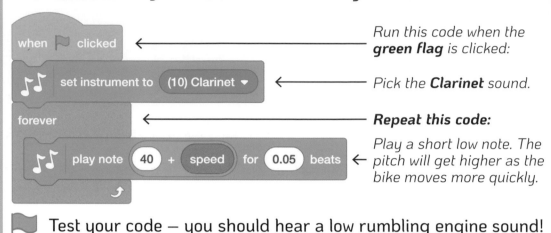

when ⚑ clicked ← *Run this code when the **green flag** is clicked:*

♪♫ set instrument to (10) Clarinet ▼ ← *Pick the **Clarinet** sound.*

forever ← ***Repeat this code:***

♪♫ play note (40 + speed) for (0.05) beats ← *Play a short low note. The pitch will get higher as the bike moves more quickly.*

⚑ Test your code — you should hear a low rumbling engine sound!

12 Speeding up

This code will make the bike speed up when the **Right arrow** key is pressed.

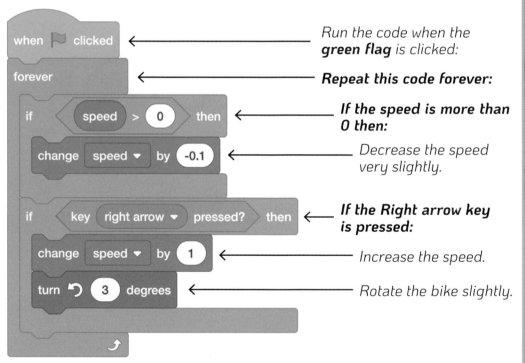

when ⚑ clicked ← *Run the code when the **green flag** is clicked:*

forever ← ***Repeat this code forever:***

if (speed > 0) then ← ***If the speed is more than 0 then:***

change speed ▼ by (-0.1) ← *Decrease the speed very slightly.*

if (key right arrow ▼ pressed?) then ← ***If the Right arrow key is pressed:***

change speed ▼ by (1) ← *Increase the speed.*

turn ↺ (3) degrees ← *Rotate the bike slightly.*

⚑ Run your code and tap the **Right** arrow key. The engine note should change and the bike should rotate a bit.

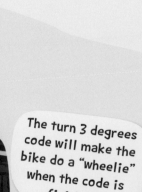

The turn 3 degrees code will make the bike do a "wheelie" when the code is finished.

The bike will slow down gradually if no keys are pressed.

13 Slowing down

When the **Left arrow** key is pressed this will operate a brake and slow the motorbike down.

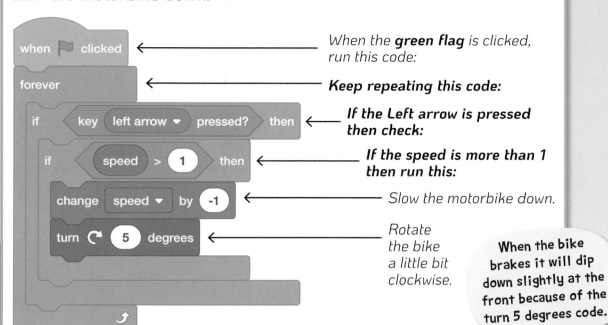

When the **green flag** is clicked, run this code:

Keep repeating this code:

If the Left arrow is pressed then check:

If the speed is more than 1 then run this:

Slow the motorbike down.

Rotate the bike a little bit clockwise.

When the bike brakes it will dip down slightly at the front because of the turn 5 degrees code.

Run your code and tap the **Right** arrow key to speed up. Try slowing down with the **Left** arrow key.

14 Make it move

This code will start the motorbike moving.

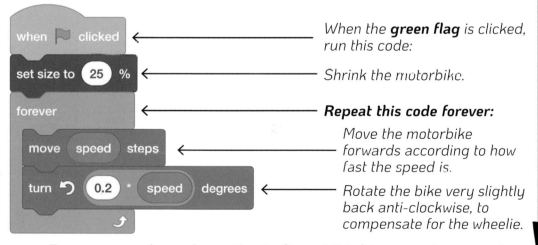

When the **green flag** is clicked, run this code:

Shrink the motorbike.

Repeat this code forever:

Move the motorbike forwards according to how fast the speed is.

Rotate the bike very slightly back anti-clockwise, to compensate for the wheelie.

Next, we need to give it something to drive on!

Run your code and use the **Left** and **Right** arrow keys to slow down and speed up. The bike should ride around the screen in a large circle.

15 Prepare the backdrop

We need to get the background ready for our game.

Click the **Stage** icon.

Click the **Backdrops** tab.

Click **Convert to Bitmap.**

16 Blue sky

Make the whole of the backdrop light blue.

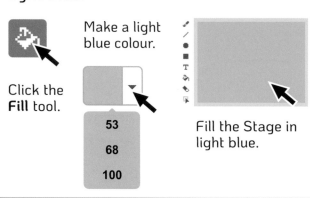

Click the **Fill** tool.

Make a light blue colour.

| 53 |
| 68 |
| 100 |

Fill the Stage in light blue.

17 Green grass

Add some grass at the bottom of the backdrop.

Choose the **Rectangle** tool.

Mix a green colour.

| 34 |
| 60 |
| 78 |

Drag out a green rectangle at the bottom of the Stage.

18 Select the bike

Click the **Sprite1** icon.

Sprite1

19 More code!

Code

Click the **Code** tab.

Later on we will add more levels to the game!

20 Get things ready

This code will reset the speed variables and make sure the motorbike is ready.

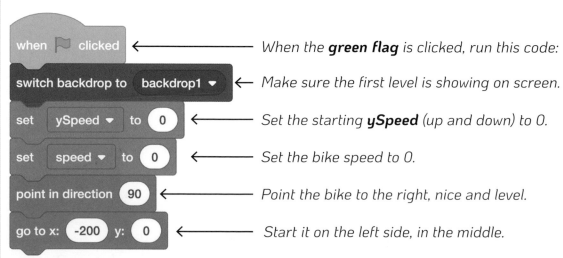

when 🚩 clicked ← *When the **green flag** is clicked, run this code:*

switch backdrop to backdrop1 ▾ ← *Make sure the first level is showing on screen.*

set ySpeed ▾ to 0 ← *Set the starting **ySpeed** (up and down) to 0.*

set speed ▾ to 0 ← *Set the bike speed to 0.*

point in direction 90 ← *Point the bike to the right, nice and level.*

go to x: -200 y: 0 ← *Start it on the left side, in the middle.*

🚩 Run the code to check the bike moves to the left, and its speed is 0.

21 Gravity!

This code simulates gravity by increasing the **ySpeed** variable and pulling the bike down. If either wheel hits the ground, the code makes them bounce up.

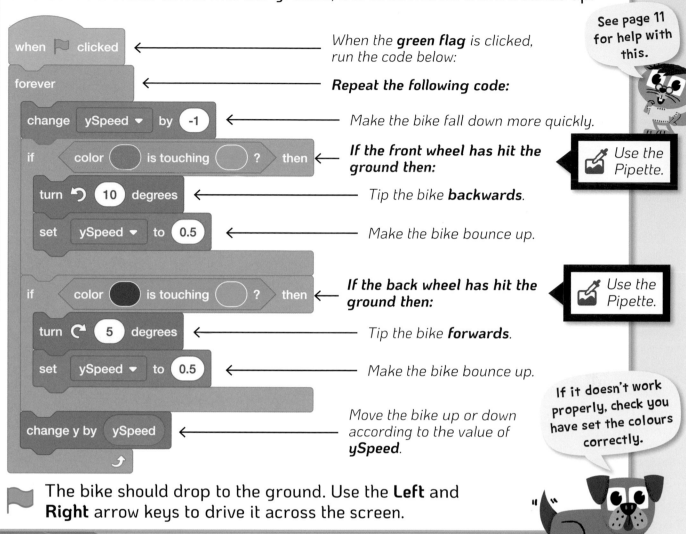

*When the **green flag** is clicked, run the code below:*

Repeat the following code:

Make the bike fall down more quickly.

If the front wheel has hit the ground then:

*Tip the bike **backwards**.*

Make the bike bounce up.

Use the Pipette.

If the back wheel has hit the ground then:

*Tip the bike **forwards**.*

Make the bike bounce up.

Use the Pipette.

*Move the bike up or down according to the value of **ySpeed**.*

See page 11 for help with this.

If it doesn't work properly, check you have set the colours correctly.

The bike should drop to the ground. Use the **Left** and **Right** arrow keys to drive it across the screen.

22 Switch to the backdrop

We're going back to drawing!

Click the **Stage** icon.

Click the **Backdrops** tab.

23 Another level

Right-click the **backdrop1** icon.

Choose **duplicate** to add another backdrop.

24 And another!

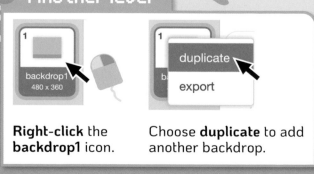

Repeat Step 23 so that you have three backdrops like this.

Click **backdrop2** to select it.

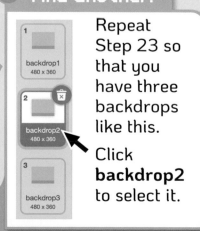

25 Design the second level

Draw a hill for the motorbike to ride up.

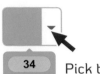 Pick the **Brush** tool.

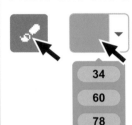 Pick the green we used before.

34
60
78

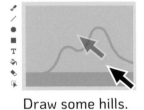 Draw a hill. Make sure there are no gaps.

 Select the **Fill** tool.

Fill in the hill.

 You could use the Pipette to set the green colour.

26 Next backdrop

Click **backdrop3** to select it.

27 Design the third level

Make this one a bit trickier than the second level.

34
60
78

Draw some hills.

Fill in the hills.

We need the correct shade of green so the code can check the wheels have hit the ground.

28 More bike code

Click the **Sprite1** icon.

Choose the **Code** tab.

Code

29 Code the levels

This code will check when the bike has completed each level by reaching the right side of the Stage.

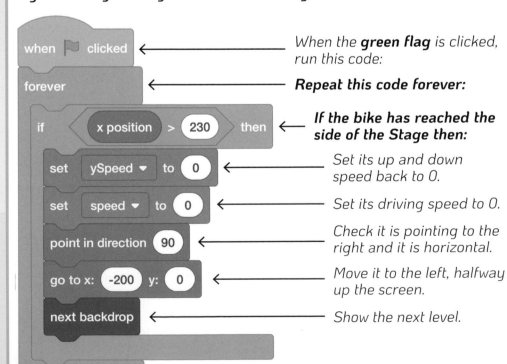

*When the **green flag** is clicked, run this code:*

Repeat this code forever:

If the bike has reached the side of the Stage then:

Set its up and down speed back to 0.

Set its driving speed to 0.

Check it is pointing to the right and it is horizontal.

Move it to the left, halfway up the screen.

Show the next level.

Our final bit of code will check if the rider has fallen off, by testing if their helmet has hit the ground.

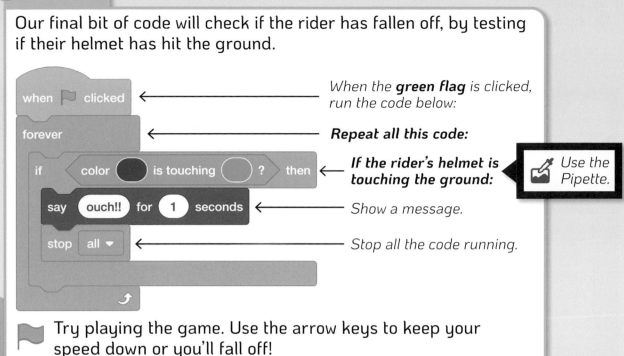

When the **green flag** is clicked, run the code below:

Repeat all this code:

If the rider's helmet is touching the ground:

Use the Pipette.

Show a message.

Stop all the code running.

Try playing the game. Use the arrow keys to keep your speed down or you'll fall off!

Challenges

Try to add levels that look like these:

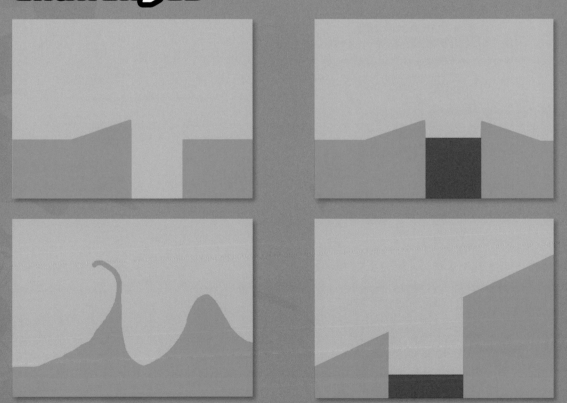

- The code in Step 21 simulates gravity. Use -2 instead of -1 and see what happens.

- Change the amount the bike rotates when you accelerate or brake, by editing the code when the **Right** or **Left** arrow keys are pressed.

- Try using different instruments to make the motorbike noise. Try different starting values instead of 40.

Parking Stur

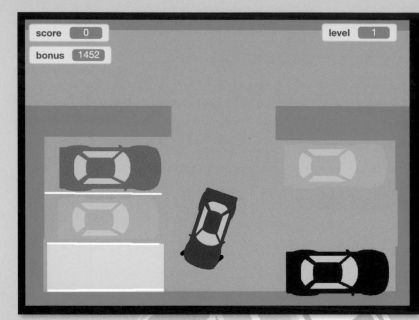

score 0
bonus 1452
level 1

You need to be good at parking a car to win at this game! We will use similar code to Track Driver to make a car move around. Additional code will make it look as though the front wheels are pointing in the correct direction. Code will check if the car has collided with other cars. Different backdrops will provide multiple levels for the game.

1 Start Scratch

Visit the Scratch website and create a new file.

C **scratch.mit.edu**

2 No cats

We won't need the cat, so click on the bin to delete it.

Sprite1

3 Add a painted sprite

Add a sprite to use as the car.

Hover

Hover over the **Choose a Sprite** button.

Don't click it!

Paint

A menu will show.

Move up to the **Paint** option and click it.

4 Bitmap

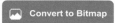
Convert to Bitmap

Click the **Convert to Bitmap** button.

Page 37 has all the steps to draw this car.

5 Draw a car from above

Draw a very large rectangle to outline the car (our code will shrink it later). **Turn back to page 37** for help drawing all the details.

Select the **Rectangle** tool then mix blue.

56
87
91

6 Add a sound effect

We need a sound effect to play when the car crashes into a parked car.

 Select the **Sounds** tab.

 Click **Choose a Sound**.

7 Find the sound

Scroll through the sounds and click on **Car Horn**.

8 Start coding!

Click the **Code** tab.

9 How fast?

Our first variable is going to store the speed of the car. Create a variable called **speed**.

 Choose the **Variables** group.

Click **Make a Variable**.

 Type **speed**.

Click **OK**.

10 Four more variables

Make four more variables called **score**, **level**, **bonus**, and **crashed**.

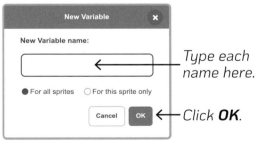 Click **Make a Variable**.

Type each name here.

Click **OK**.

 Tick the variables you want on screen.

Make sure all five variables show here.

11 Forwards and backwards

This code will make the car drive forwards or backwards when the A or Z keys are pressed.

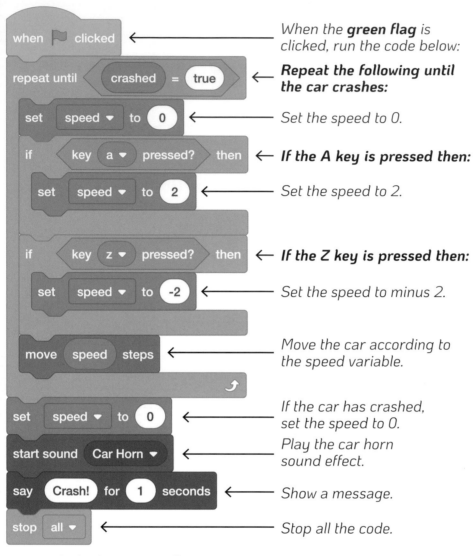

when ⚑ clicked ← *When the **green flag** is clicked, run the code below:*

repeat until ⟨ crashed = true ⟩ ← ***Repeat the following until the car crashes:***

set speed ▾ to 0 ← *Set the speed to 0.*

if ⟨ key a ▾ pressed? ⟩ then ← ***If the A key is pressed then:***

set speed ▾ to 2 ← *Set the speed to 2.*

if ⟨ key z ▾ pressed? ⟩ then ← ***If the Z key is pressed then:***

set speed ▾ to -2 ← *Set the speed to minus 2.*

move speed steps ← *Move the car according to the speed variable.*

set speed ▾ to 0 ← *If the car has crashed, set the speed to 0.*

start sound Car Horn ▾ ← *Play the car horn sound effect.*

say Crash! for 1 seconds ← *Show a message.*

stop all ▾ ← *Stop all the code.*

⚑ Click the **green flag** then try moving the car with the A and Z keys.

12 Click Costumes

Click the **Costumes** tab.

🖌 Costumes

We need three different versions of the car.

They will show the car going forwards, left or right.

14 Another costume

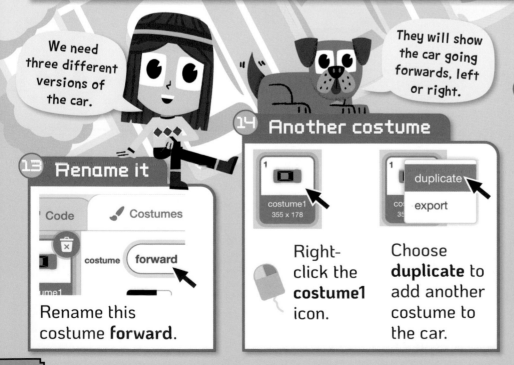

Right-click the **costume1** icon.

Choose **duplicate** to add another costume to the car.

13 Rename it

Code 🖌 Costumes

costume forward

Rename this costume **forward**.

15 And another

Repeat Steps 12 and 13 so that you have three costumes like this.

Click the middle one to select it.

1 forward 390 x 186
2 forward2 390 x 186
3 forward3 390 x 186

56

16 Draw the car steering left

As the car steers left, the front tyres will stick out.

Choose the **Line** tool.

Pick black.

Zoom in on the **top right** of the costume.

Draw the tyre. Make sure there are no gaps.

Select the **Fill** tool.

Fill in the tyre.

Zoom in on the **bottom right**.

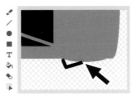

Draw the tyre. No gaps!

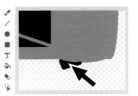

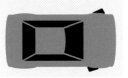

Fill in the tyre.

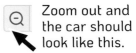

Zoom out and the car should look like this.

costume Rename the costume **left**.

17 Select the third costume

Click the **third costume** to select it.

18 Draw the car steering left

Now, draw the car steering right. The front tyres will stick out the opposite way.

Zoom in on the **top right** of the costume.

Draw the tyre.

Fill it in.

Zoom in on the **bottom right**.

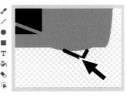

Draw the tyre.

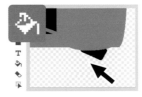

Fill it in.

costume **right**

Rename this costume **right**.

Zoom out and the car should look like this.

The three costumes should now look like this.

⑲ Code the steering

This code will steer the car when the arrow keys are used. It will also show the correct costume so it looks like the car is actually steering!

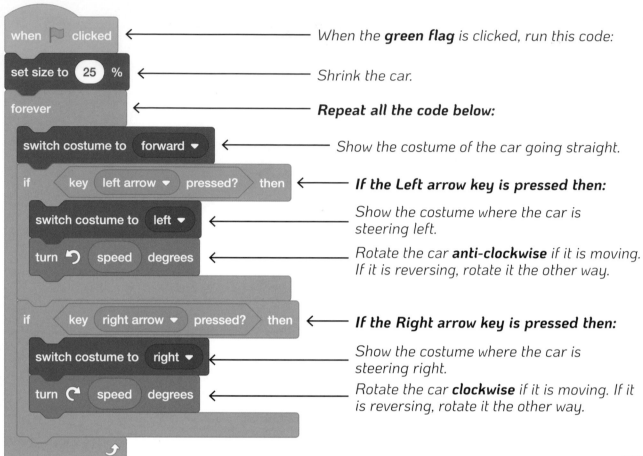

When the **green flag** is clicked, run this code:

Shrink the car.

Repeat all the code below:

Show the costume of the car going straight.

If the Left arrow key is pressed then:

Show the costume where the car is steering left.

Rotate the car **anti-clockwise** if it is moving. If it is reversing, rotate it the other way.

If the Right arrow key is pressed then:

Show the costume where the car is steering right.

Rotate the car **clockwise** if it is moving. If it is reversing, rotate it the other way.

🚩 Try driving the car. Hold down the A key, then press the arrow keys to turn left or right.

Remember, the car must be moving for the steering to work!

⑳ Add a sound

We will pick some music to play in the background.

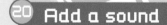

Select the **Sounds** tab.

Click **Choose a Sound**.

㉑ Pick the music

Dance Chill..

Scroll through the sounds and select **Dance Chill Out**.

22 Code the background music

This code will play the background music over and over, getting slightly quicker and higher pitched.

When the **green flag** is clicked, start this code:

Repeat all the following code:

Play the music.

Make the music play at a very slightly higher pitch and faster speed.

🚩 Drive around and listen to the music!

23 Draw the background

We need somewhere for the car to drive.

Click the **Stage** icon.

Click the **Backdrops** tab.

Click on **Convert to Bitmap.**

24 Green grass

Make the whole of the backdrop green.

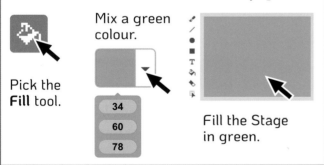

Pick the **Fill** tool.

Mix a green colour.

34
60
78

Fill the Stage in green.

25 Start the car park

Use rectangles to make a simple space.

Choose the **Rectangle** tool.

Mix grey for the road.

0
0
89

Draw the car park with rectangles.

If you make a mistake, click Undo!

Complete the car park.

18
53
100

Make a light yellow colour.

Draw a rectangle for the car to park on.

0
0
100

Mix white.

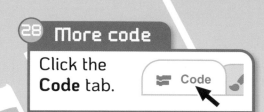

Add some lines to the car park.

27 **Select the car sprite**

Click **Sprite1**.

Sprite1

28 **More code**

Click the **Code** tab.

Code

29 **Check if the car has been parked**

We need to test if the car has been parked properly. We will check if the car is touching the light yellow colour. It needs to be fully on the yellow rectangle *and* not touching the grey.

See page 11 for help with the Pipette.

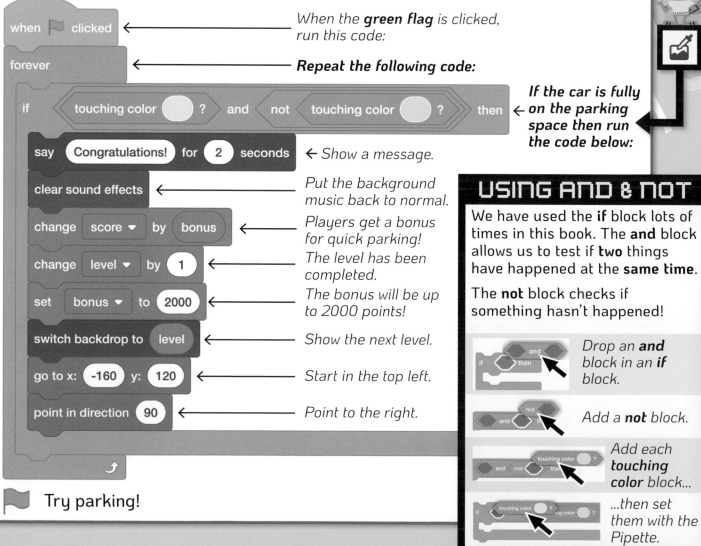

When the green flag is clicked, run this code:

when ⚑ clicked

forever

Repeat the following code:

if ⟨ touching color ⬤ ? ⟩ and ⟨ not ⟨ touching color ⬤ ? ⟩ ⟩ then

If the car is fully on the parking space then run the code below:

say Congratulations! for 2 seconds   ← *Show a message.*

clear sound effects   ← *Put the background music back to normal.*

change score ▾ by bonus   ← *Players get a bonus for quick parking!*

change level ▾ by 1   ← *The level has been completed.*

set bonus ▾ to 2000   ← *The bonus will be up to 2000 points!*

switch backdrop to level   ← *Show the next level.*

go to x: -160 y: 120   ← *Start in the top left.*

point in direction 90   ← *Point to the right.*

⚑ Try parking!

USING AND & NOT

We have used the **if** block lots of times in this book. The **and** block allows us to test if **two** things have happened at the **same time**.

The **not** block checks if something hasn't happened!

*Drop an **and** block in an **if** block.*

*Add a **not** block.*

*Add each **touching color** block...*

...then set them with the Pipette.

30 Click Costumes

Click the **Costumes** tab.

31 Copy the car picture

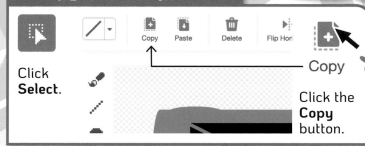

Click **Select**.

Copy

Click the **Copy** button.

Can you guess where we will paste this car picture?

32 Backdrop

Select the Stage so we can see the car park.

Click the **Stage** icon.

33 Add another level

Right-click the **backdrop1** icon.

Choose **duplicate** to add another backdrop.

34 Add a car to the car park

Choose the **Select** tool. Paste the car in and make it smaller.

Click **Select**.

Paste

Click **Paste**.

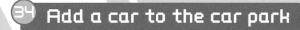

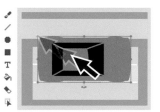

Drag one of the corner handles to shrink the car.

Make it a bit smaller...

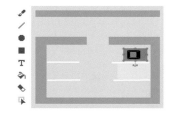

...until it is roughly the same size as the other car.

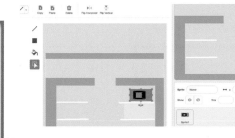

Look on the stage to compare the sizes.

35 Respray

Change the colour of the new car to red.

Pick the **Fill** tool.

Mix a red colour.

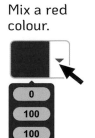

0
100
100

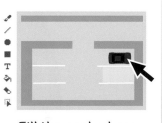

Fill the parked car in red.

61

More car code

Click the **Sprite1** icon.   Choose the **Code** tab.

Start up code

This code gets everything ready for the start of the game.

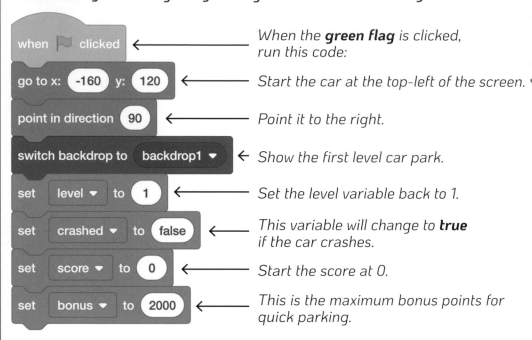

When the **green flag** is clicked, run this code:

Start the car at the top-left of the screen.

Point it to the right.

Show the first level car park.

Set the level variable back to 1.

This variable will change to **true** if the car crashes.

Start the score at 0.

This is the maximum bonus points for quick parking.

Add this short section of code to decrease the bonus the player gets for quick parking:

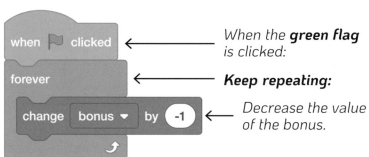

When the **green flag** is clicked:

Keep repeating:

Decrease the value of the bonus.

If your car keeps starting on the grass, the game won't work.

If that happens, change the go to x and y values or make the grey road bigger.

Drive carefully!

Add this code to check if the car hits the grass or a parked car:

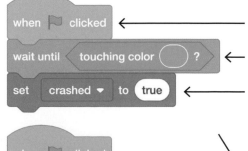

When the **green flag** is clicked:

Do nothing unless the car hits the green grass.

This will stop the main loop and end the game.

This code will keep waiting for the player's car to crash into the red car. If it does, the game will end.

Test the game!

Try parking the car. After you manage the first level, the next level should start automatically. Mind the other cars!

You need to add code like this for each colour of car you add to the car park. Remember to use the Pipette!

Challenges

Try to add more levels like these. You will need to repeat Steps 33 to 35. If you add different coloured cars then add another section of code from the second part of Step 37 for each colour. Change red to the colour of each car so that the code is testing whether the player has collided with each car.

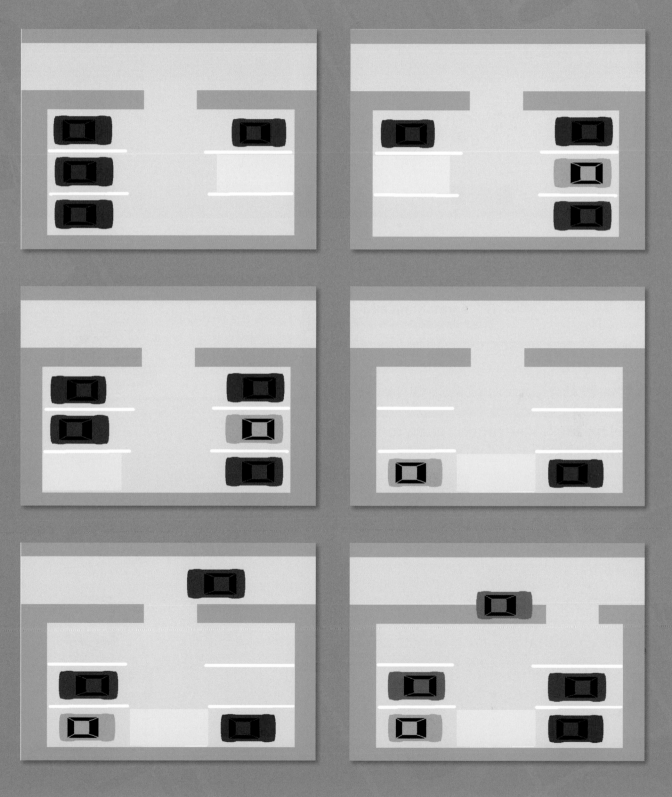

3D Driver

score 0
speed 125
timer 14.223

Although this game doesn't really show 3D, it introduces the idea of showing perspective. This means the cars that are further away need to appear smaller than the ones that are near to the player's car. This is done by changing the size of car sprites according to their y value. Each car is cloned using similar code to the Formula Racer game.

1 Start Scratch

Go to the Scratch website and create a new file.

C **scratch.mit.edu**

2 Too fast for cats

Click on the bin to delete the cat sprite.

Sprite1

3 Prepare the background

Get the background ready for our game.

🖌 Backdrops

📷 Convert to Bitmap

Click the **Backdrops** tab.

Click on **Convert to Bitmap**.

Look for the centre target!

4 Draw the track

Draw the road that the cars will race down.

Choose the **Line** tool.

Mix a light grey.

58
1
82

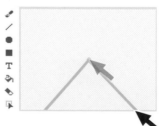

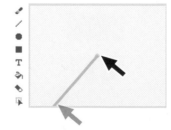

Fill it in.

Draw two lines to the centre to make a triangle.

Draw the sky

To give the game more perspective we will use a rectangle filled with a blend of two colours.

Pick the **Rectangle** tool.

Select the **Vertical Gradient** fill option.

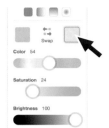
Set the first colour to be **53-68-100**.

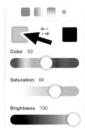
Set the second colour to be **54-24-100**.

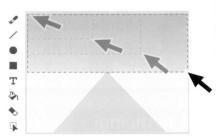
Drag down a rectangle from the top-left corner to make the sky.

 **Draw the grass**

We will use a similar method to blend the colour for the grass.

Select the **Fill** tool.

Pick the **Vertical Gradient** fill option.

Set the first colour to be **25-50-100**.

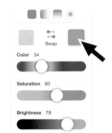
Set the second colour to be **34-60-78**.

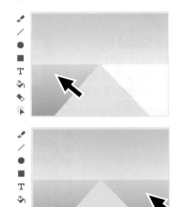
Click to fill in the grass.

---

7 Start coding!

Click the **Code** tab.

---

8 The speed

Create a variable called **speed**.

Choose the **Variables** group.

Click **Make a Variable**.

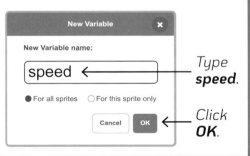

Type **speed**.

Click **OK**.

---

9 The score

Make a second variable called **score**.

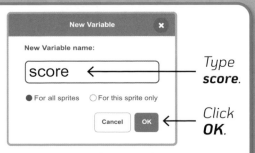

Click **Make a Variable**.

Type **score**.

Click **OK**.

The faster the player drives, the more points they will get!

More and more cars!

This code will clone another copy of the car every second!

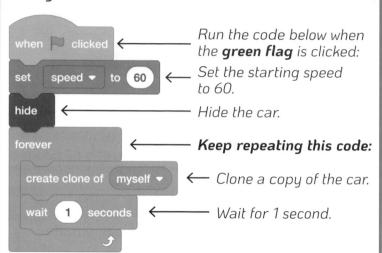

Run the code below when the **green flag** is clicked:

Set the starting speed to 60.

Hide the car.

Keep repeating this code:

Clone a copy of the car.

Wait for 1 second.

CREATING PERSPECTIVE

Perspective is a way of making a flat 2D image look 3D and more real. In this game we will create perspective by making the computer's cars get bigger as they get closer to the player's car.

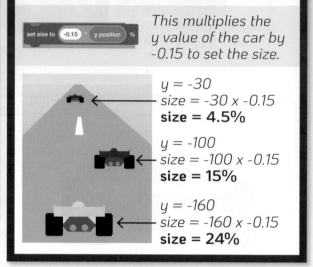

This multiplies the y value of the car by -0.15 to set the size.

$y = -30$
$size = -30 \times -0.15$
size = 4.5%

$y = -100$
$size = -100 \times -0.15$
size = 15%

$y = -160$
$size = -160 \times -0.15$
size = 24%

19 **Move each car**

After each clone is made, this code will randomise them and make them move down the screen.

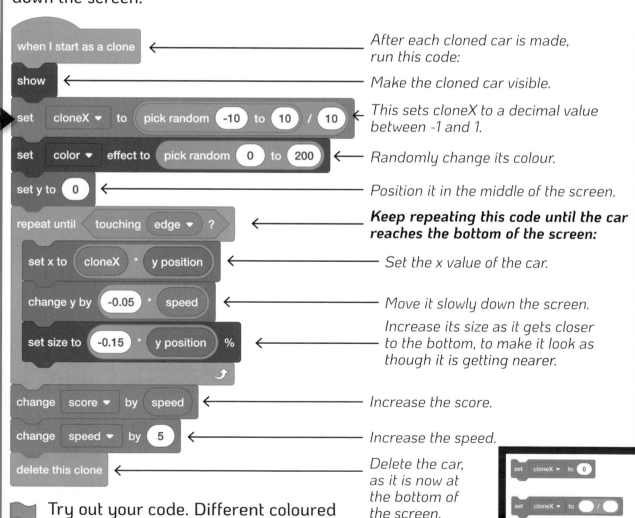

After each cloned car is made, run this code:

Make the cloned car visible.

This sets cloneX to a decimal value between -1 and 1.

Randomly change its colour.

Position it in the middle of the screen.

Keep repeating this code until the car reaches the bottom of the screen:

Set the x value of the car.

Move it slowly down the screen.

Increase its size as it gets closer to the bottom, to make it look as though it is getting nearer.

Increase the score.

Increase the speed.

Delete the car, as it is now at the bottom of the screen.

Try out your code. Different coloured cars should start moving down the screen.

20 Import the Music extension

We'll use the **Music** extension blocks to create our sound effects.

Click the **Add Extension** button.

Choose the **Music** extension.

21 Deal with collisions

Each cloned car needs to check if it has hit the player's car — Sprite1.

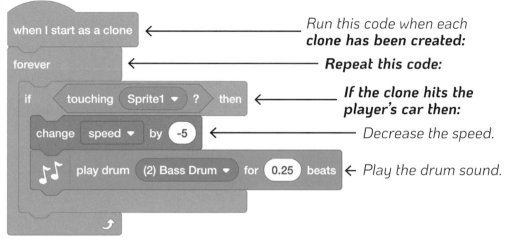

when I start as a clone ← *Run this code when each* ***clone has been created:***

forever ← ***Repeat this code:***

if touching Sprite1 ▼ ? then ← ***If the clone hits the player's car then:***

change speed ▼ by -5 ← *Decrease the speed.*

play drum (2) Bass Drum ▼ for 0.25 beats ← *Play the drum sound.*

⚑ Test the code. Every time the cars collide, a drum will sound and they will all slow down.

22 Select the first car

Click the **Sprite1** icon.

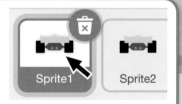

23 Code the engine sound

This code will create an engine noise. As the speed changes, the pitch will get higher.

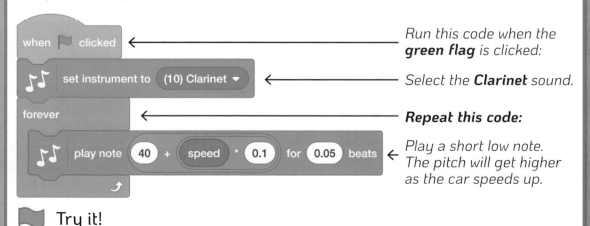

when ⚑ clicked ← *Run this code when the* ***green flag*** *is clicked:*

set instrument to (10) Clarinet ▼ ← *Select the **Clarinet** sound.*

forever ← ***Repeat this code:***

play note 40 + speed * 0.1 for 0.05 beats ← *Play a short low note. The pitch will get higher as the car speeds up.*

⚑ Try it!

Grrrrr!

24 Steer left and right

Add this code to steer the car left and right when the arrow keys are pressed.

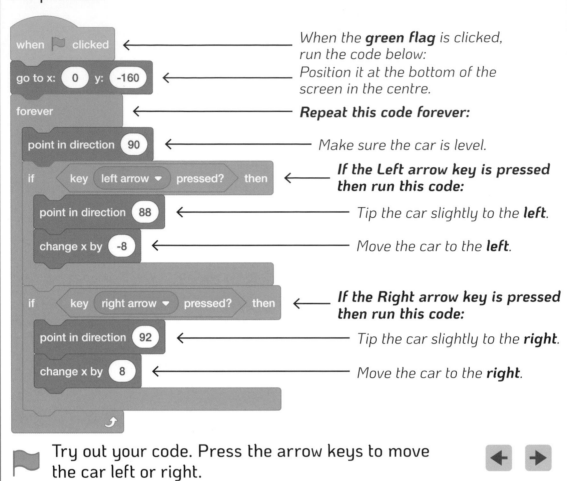

*When the **green flag** is clicked, run the code below:*
Position it at the bottom of the screen in the centre.

Repeat this code forever:

Make sure the car is level.

If the Left arrow key is pressed then run this code:

*Tip the car slightly to the **left**.*

*Move the car to the **left**.*

If the Right arrow key is pressed then run this code:

*Tip the car slightly to the **right**.*

*Move the car to the **right**.*

Try out your code. Press the arrow keys to move the car left or right.

25 Stop the game!

If the speed slows down then the game needs to stop.

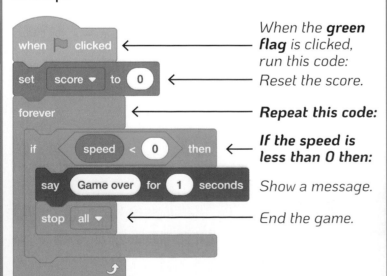

*When the **green flag** is clicked, run this code:*
Reset the score.

Repeat this code:

If the speed is less than 0 then:

Show a message.

End the game.

26 Stay on track!

Add this code to slow down the car if it touches the green grass.

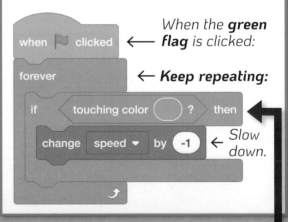

*When the **green flag** is clicked:*

← Keep repeating:

Slow down.

Use the Pipette to pick the shade of green near the car.

27 Out of time

Use this code to stop the game after 30 seconds.

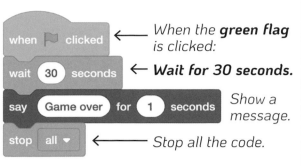

When the **green flag** is clicked:

Wait for 30 seconds.

Show a message.

Stop all the code.

🚩 How many points can you score before the time runs out?

28 Add a sprite

This sprite will show the road markings.

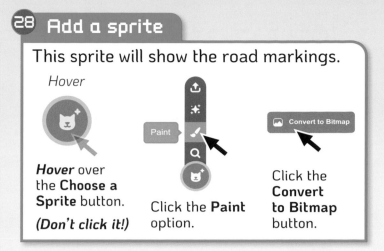

Hover

Hover over the **Choose a Sprite** button. *(Don't click it!)*

Click the **Paint** option.

Click the **Convert to Bitmap** button.

29 White line

Draw a line on the road.

Mix white.

0
0
100

Fill in the shape.

The white line needs to be this shape to give a sense of perspective.

30 Move the line

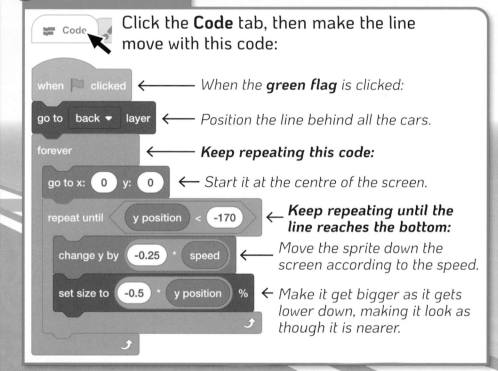

Click the **Code** tab, then make the line move with this code:

When the **green flag** is clicked:

Position the line behind all the cars.

Keep repeating this code:

Start it at the centre of the screen.

Keep repeating until the line reaches the bottom:

Move the sprite down the screen according to the speed.

Make it get bigger as it gets lower down, making it look as though it is nearer.

Challenges

- Make the speed increase more quickly (see Step 19).
- Change what happens when the cars collide.
- It can be tricky to avoid the cars as the speed goes up. Try changing the size set in Step 19 to make them smaller. You also need to change the size of the player's car.
- Add a tree sprite to the track. Use the ideas from Step 30 to make it change size.

Game Challenges: Monster Truck

You need to have coded the whole of Motorcross Rider to make this game.

If you have built Motorcross Rider you can adapt your project to make a monster truck game. Instead of a motorbike, a massive monster truck will have to drive over hills and obstacles!

You need to have a Scratch account and be logged in to do this.

1 Make a copy of the game

Sign in to Scratch and make a copy of Motorcross Rider.

Click the **Folder** icon to load your saved files.

My Stuff

Track Racer
See inside

Motorcross Rider
See inside

Find where you saved Motorcross Rider and click **See Inside**.

File Edit

New
Save now
Save as a copy

Click **Save as a copy**.

Monster Trucks

Rename your project then click **File > Save now**.

2 New costume

Add a new costume to **Sprite1** (the bike).

Paint

Convert to Bitmap

3 Draw a monster truck!

Use the drawing techniques you have learnt about from the other projects.

Make the wheels the same colour as the motorbike's wheels.

4 Test your game

Make any final changes then test your game!

Add the same blue as the rider's helmet on the roof of the truck.

This will stop the game if the truck turns over.

5 Your own ideas

Why not set your game in the desert — or even on the moon!

Modify the code so the truck wheels stop when they touch yellow.

Game Challenge: 3D Motorbike Racer

You need to have coded the whole of 3D Driver to make this game.

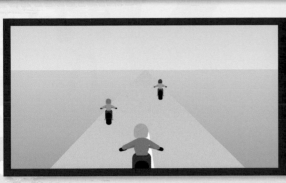

Once you have coded 3D Driver, why not adapt that project and make a motorbike racing game? Motorbikes will replace the cars as you guide your way though the pack to win the race!

If you saved the game on your computer, you can just load it, rename it and save it again.

1 Make a copy of the game

Sign in to Scratch and make a copy of 3D Driver.

Click the **Folder** icon to load your saved files.

My Stuff

Track Racer
See inside

3D Driver
See inside

Find where you saved 3D Driver and click **See inside**.

File Edit
New
Save now
Save as a copy

Click **Save as a copy**.

3D bike racer

Rename your project then click **File > Save now**.

2 New costume

Add a new costume to **Sprite1**.

Paint

3 Draw a motorbike

Draw the rear view — from behind.

4 Make a copy

Copy the costume to use on the other sprite.

Choose the **Select** tool.

Copy

Click **Copy**.

See page 61 for help with copy and paste.

5 Select Sprite2

Click **Sprite2** to select it.

Sprite1   Sprite2

6 New costume

Add a new costume to **Sprite2**.

Remember to click Convert to Bitmap!

7 Paste and race!

Paste the motorbike picture into Sprite2.

Paste

Click **Paste**.

🚩 Test your game!

Edit your code to change how far the motorbikes lean when you move left or right.

Game Mods

After you have coded a game and tried the challenges there are still lots of extra things you can add to make your game even better! In this section there are some exciting ways to modify your driving games. Experiment and have fun with your code.

Before you start using this section, load a game you have finished coding. Then, choose one of the mods to use.

> Mods are ways to change a game. Mods is short for modifications.

A: Uploading Images

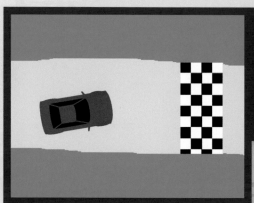

You have learnt how to create your own images for most of the games. But maybe you want to use a graphic from the web or a photo of a real car? Here's how to add them into your games.

> Sometimes it helps if you add the word "transparent" to your search.

A1 Find an image

Go online and search for an image to use. Some games need the car to be shown from above; some from the side.

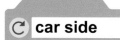

⟳ **car above**   or   ⟳ **car side**

A2 Choose one

Pick one image and click it.

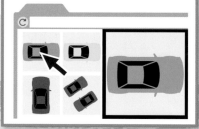

A3 Download it

Find the large version of the image.

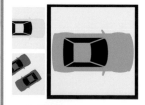

Right-click the image.

Choose **Save Image As...**

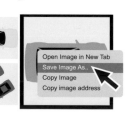

Open Image in New Tab
Save Image As...
Copy Image
Copy image address

Save as: green car.png   **Save**

📁 Documents ←

homework.doc

Save it in your Documents folder.

Save

Click **Save**.

A4 Open your game

Go to Scratch and find your game. Click on the sprite you want to add the image to.

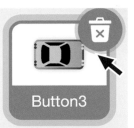

Button3

A5 Click upload

Upload the image to the sprite as a new costume.

Click the **Costumes** tab.

Hover over the **Choose a Costume** button.

Click **Upload Costume**.

A6 Upload it!

💳 Desktop	**green car.png**
📁 Documents	homework.doc
⬇ Downloads	racing car.png
	rocket.png

Find the file and double-click it.

Your sprite should now change into the image you chose.

🏁 Test your code.

> Change the number in the set size block to resize your image so it fits your game.

B) Speedo

In any of the games that use a speed variable you can add a speedometer! This uses two sprites – a black circle as a dial, and a red needle. The red needle turns round to an angle based on the current speed.

B1 Add a painted sprite

Start by loading one of your games. Add a new sprite to be the dial.

Hover

Hover over the **Choose a Sprite** button.

Paint

Move up to the **Paint** option and click it.

B2 Bitmap

🖼 Convert to Bitmap

Click the **Convert to Bitmap** button.

B3 Start drawing!

Start by drawing the dial.

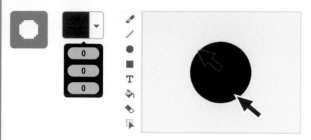

Draw a circle in the centre of the drawing area.

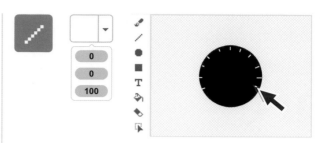

Add some lines around the edge of the speedo.

B4 Final touches

Add any final details to the dial.

B5 Add another sprite

Repeat steps B1 and B2 to add the sprite.

 Paint

 Convert to Bitmap

B6 Draw the needle

Now, draw the needle that points to the current speed.

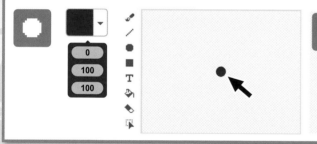

B7 Code the needle

Drag this code in to make the speedo work:

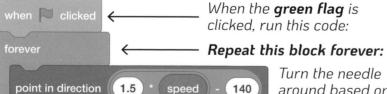

when 🏳 clicked ⟵ *When the **green flag** is clicked, run this code:*

forever ⟵ ***Repeat this block forever:***

point in direction (1.5 * speed) - 140

Turn the needle around based on the speed value.

🏳 Try out your mod.

> Change these values to make the speedo fit your game.

> If the needle doesn't turn enough, change 1.5 to a bigger number, like 10.

[] High Score

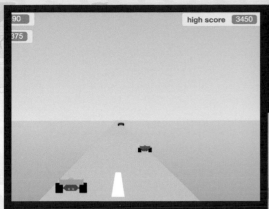

This mod adds a high score to any game that uses a score variable. At the end of a game it will check the current score and see if it is bigger than the previous high score.

C1 Make a variable

Create a variable called **high score**.

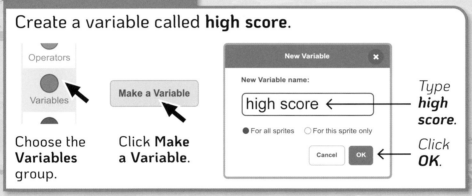

Choose the **Variables** group.

Click **Make a Variable**.

Type **high score**.

Click **OK**.

C2 Code it

Add this code to your game. It needs to go right at the end, *after* any "game over" messages:

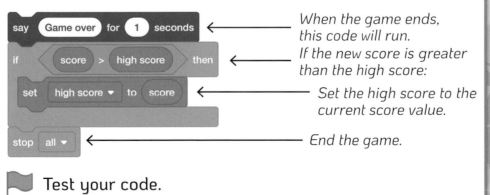

When the game ends, this code will run.

If the new score is greater than the high score:

Set the high score to the current score value.

End the game.

🚩 Test your code.

Some games, like 3D Driver, have more than one "game over" and "stop" command in the code.

Therefore, you may need to add the code twice – after each "say game over" block.

D) Lap Timer

Racing car drivers qualify for races by competing to see who can set the fastest lap time. This mod adds a timer to the Track Driver and Big Track Racer games. It also displays a list of previous lap times.

D1 Show the timer

Start by showing the timer on screen.

Pick the **Sensing** group.

Click the box next to the **timer** block.

D2 Backdrop

Select the backdrop so we can edit it.

Click the **Stage** icon.

Click the **Backdrops** tab.

D3 Start drawing!

Draw a timing beam across the start line.

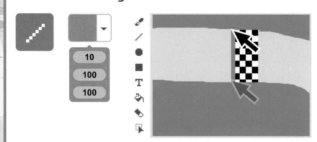

D4 The car

Click the car icon.

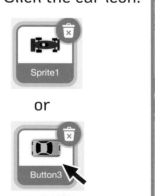

or

D5 Make a list

Create a list to store the lap times in.

Choose the **Variables** group.

Click **Make a List**.

Type **lap times**.

Click **OK**.

Click Code

Click the **Code** tab.

D7 **Code the lap timer**

Add this code to time each lap the car makes:

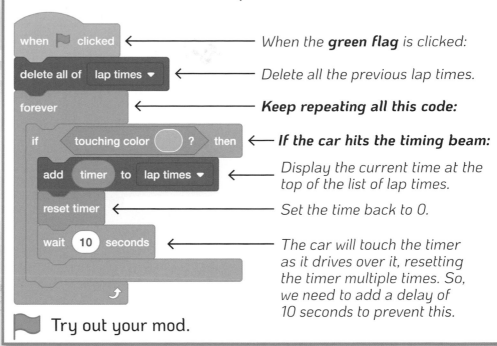

when 🏁 clicked ← *When the **green flag** is clicked:*

delete all of lap times ▾ ← *Delete all the previous lap times.*

forever ← ***Keep repeating all this code:***

if ⟨ touching color ⬤ ? ⟩ then ← ***If the car hits the timing beam:***

add timer to lap times ▾ ← *Display the current time at the top of the list of lap times.*

reset timer ← *Set the time back to 0.*

wait 10 seconds ← *The car will touch the timer as it drives over it, resetting the timer multiple times. So, we need to add a delay of 10 seconds to prevent this.*

🏁 Try out your mod.

E) 3-2-1-Countdown

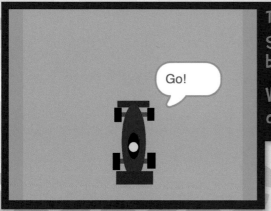

Go!

This mod builds up the tension at the start of a game. Add some code so the game says "3-2-1-Go!" before the game starts.

We will use a wait block to make some other parts of the game wait until it says go.

Don't use this on code that just makes sound effects, so the sound starts first!

E1 **Add the code**

Insert this code straight after a **when green flag clicked** block.

```
when 🏁 clicked
say 3 for 1 seconds
say 2 for 1 seconds
say 1 for 1 seconds
say Go! for 1 seconds
```

E2 **Stop other code**

🏁 Try out your mod.

You will find other parts of the code start running before your countdown is complete. Add **wait 4 seconds** after all the other **when green flag clicked** blocks.

```
when 🏁 clicked
wait 4 seconds
```

🏁 Try again!

Don't add "wait" after any "when I start as a clone" blocks.

Glossary

Accelerate Moving more and more quickly.

Algorithm A set of rules or steps to make a game or program work.

Backdrop A background picture in Scratch that shows behind the rest of your game and doesn't move.

Bitmap A way to store a graphic on a computer as a grid of tiny dots or pixels.

Block A command in Scratch that is dragged around to create code.

Code A series of commands or instructions.

Command An instruction or block that tells the computer to do something.

Coordinates The position of a sprite on the Stage, set by X and Y values.

Costume Each sprite in Scratch can have several pictures or costumes.

Duplicate Make a copy of some code or a sprite.

Gradient In graphics, this means blending two colours or shades together so that the shade changes gradually from one colour to the other.

Level A section or challenge within a computer game.

Loop A way of repeating a section of code a number of times.

Nudge To move part of an image by a small amount with the cursor keys.

Pixel One of the millions of tiny dots on a computer screen, combined together to show text, graphics or videos.

Program A set of commands that join together to make something happen.

Random A number that cannot be guessed or predicted.

Right-click Clicking the right-hand mouse button on part of the screen.

Scroll Moving objects gradually across or down the screen.

Sensing A type of block used by Scratch to test things — for example, to test if a sprite is touching a particular colour.

Sprite One of the objects in Scratch that moves around the Stage.

Stage The area of the Scratch screen that contains sprites and backdrops.

Variable A number or piece of information that can change while a program is running, such as the score in a game.